ACE YOUR MACROECONOMICS

WITH MODEL EXPLANATIONS AND EVALUATIONS

Kelvin Hong
Samuel Tay

First Printing: 2016

ISBN 978-981-09-8304-8

Edventures Pte Ltd

Singapore

www.TheEconomicsTutor.com

Acknowledgments

This work would not have been possible without the help of Lee Vint Seng, Marissa Chok and Lim Wei Jie who provided valuable inputs and helped in reviewing and editing the work.

PREFACE

This book addresses many possible questions across the entire Macroeconomics syllabus and was created to provide students with top quality explanations, diagrams, examples, evaluations, insights and expert tips to excel in their examinations.

Very often, students are unable to provide step-by-step explanations and relevant evaluation points, which are essential to scoring in examinations.

By studying the explanations provided in this book, students will also be able to better understand the various economic concepts covered in the Macroeconomics syllabus. The powerful diagrammatic analyses provided will also train students to illustrate economic concepts logically, and enable them to use such diagrams for analyses in a more effective and concise manner.

Expert tips have also been added to help the students better remember, understand and apply significant concepts, as well as avoid common errors and misconceptions.

We hope that this book will help all readers better appreciate what they are learning and excel in their Macroeconomics examinations.

Kelvin Hong
Samuel Tay

CONTENTS

1. **Explain why economic growth is desirable using the PPC and discuss whether economic growth can solve the problem of scarcity.**

The Production Possibility Curve shows the **maximum attainable combination** of goods and services that can be produced in an economy when all available **resources are fully and efficiently employed** at a fixed state of technology. **Scarcity refers to** the central problem of economics where there are **limited resources** but **unlimited human wants**. Because of Scarcity, Opportunity Cost is incurred when we make choices. Economic growth refers to the **increase in an economy's Gross Domestic Product (GDP), or total output, over time.**

Capital Goods

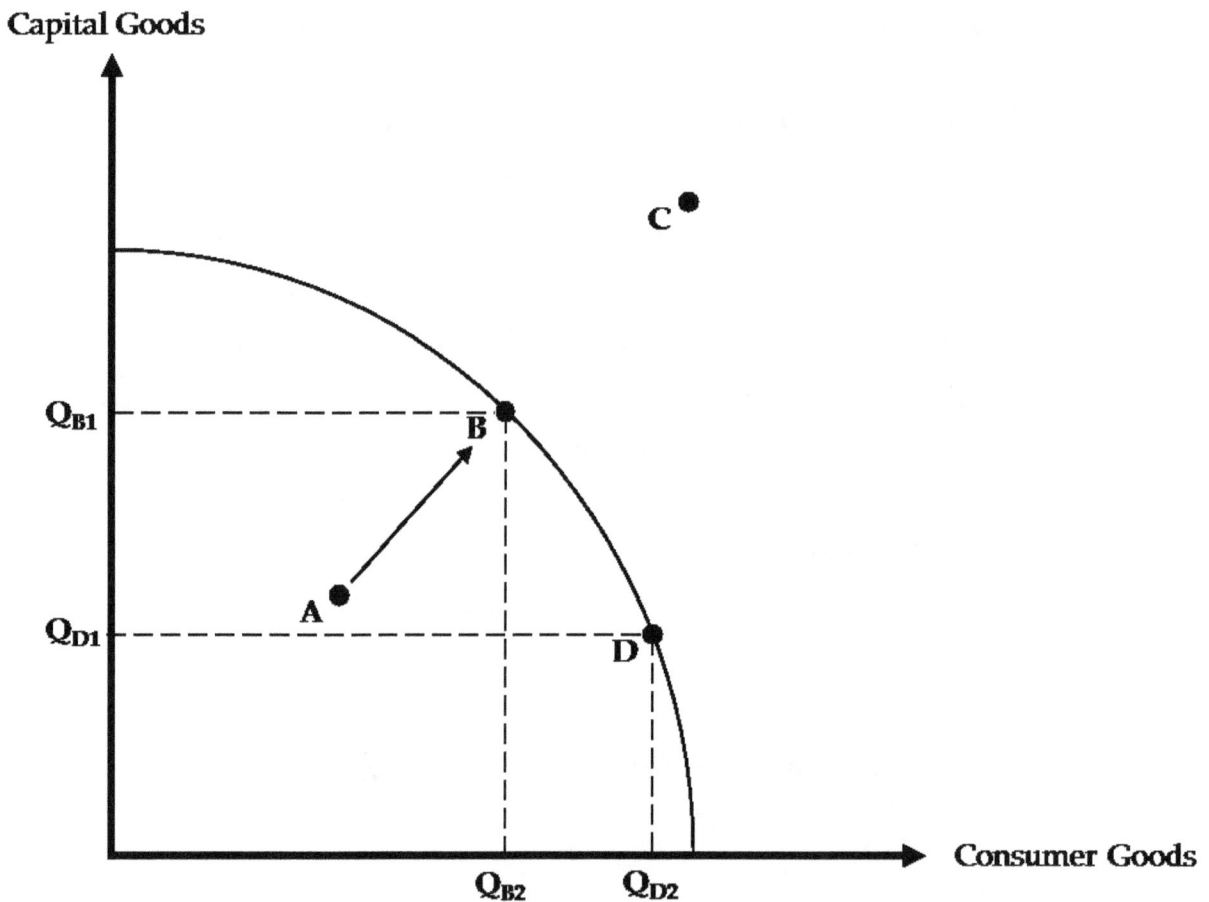

Fig 1: Actual Growth Using PPC

6

When an economy experiences **actual growth,** it means that they **are better utilising existing resources, increasing employment and producing more goods and services.** This is represented by a **movement from a point within the PPC outwards** as shown in Fig 1, with point A moving outwards towards point B. An economy can continue to **experience actual growth until it reaches its production possibility frontier.** This is the point where all available resources are being used up and there is no spare capacity to further increase output. At this point, factors of production can be redeployed to change the proportion of consumption goods and capital goods, and this is represented by a movement along the PPC.

Actual growth is desirable because it means that society is making use of available resources and producing more output to satisfy more wants. This means that material SOL increases as more goods and services are available for consumption. Hence, in achieving actual growth, the **problem of scarcity is alleviated.**

However, **total output can never go beyond that marked out by the PPC** as the PPC represents the maximum attainable combination of goods, hence despite now producing more goods and services at point B in Fig 1, the economy still cannot produce at point C, demonstrating scarcity – as there are still wants that cannot be satisfied due to the limited resources.

Staying on the PPC, choosing to produce a greater quantity of Q_{D2} of consumer goods at point D instead of Q_{B2} at point B in Fig 1 will mean that scarce resources are diverted away from the production of capital goods. Hence there is a fall in the quantity of capital goods produced from Q_{B1} to Q_{D1}, which is the opportunity cost of producing $Q_{B2}Q_{D2}$ more consumer goods.

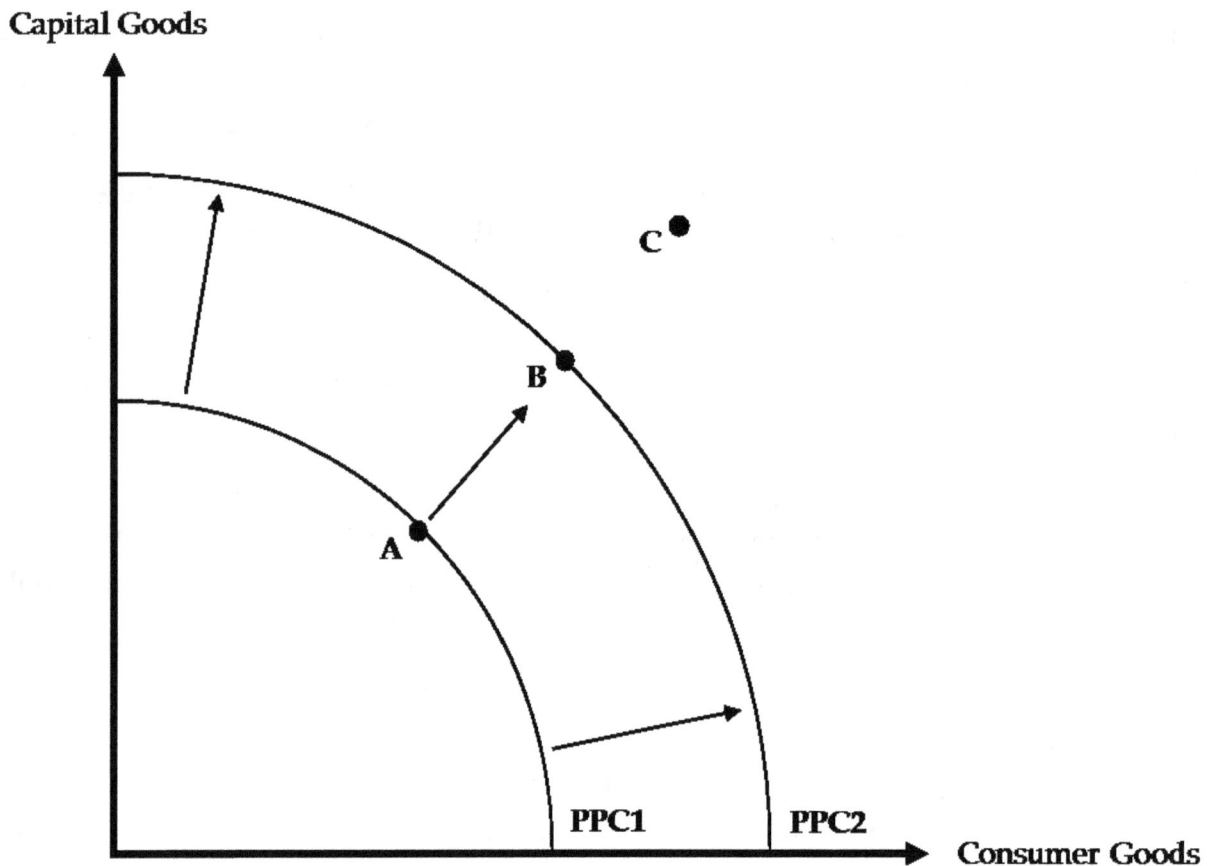

Fig 2: Potential Growth Using PPC

Potential growth refers to the **increase in the productive capacity** of the economy over time. As the productive capacity increases, we are hence able to produce more consumption goods and capital goods than before. This is represented by an outward shift of the PPC from PPC$_1$ to PPC$_2$ in Fig 2. This can be achieved as the quality or quantity of resources in the economy increases, or with advancement in the state of technology. For example, as more capital goods are added to the economy, the amount of resources would have increased since capital goods are factors of production. Therefore, the productive capacity of the economy increases.

Initially, despite actual growth in the economy, the maximum possible output of consumption and capital goods is **constrained by PPC$_1$**. It is impossible to produce and consume at levels outside of PPC$_1$. This level of **previously unattainable production** is represented by point B. However, with potential growth, the economy **experiences a**

growth in her productive capacity and is hence able to **produce more consumption goods and capital goods than before**. This is represented by an outward shift in PPC from PPC$_1$ to PPC$_2$. Hence, **point B, which was previously an unattainable combination of consumption goods and capital goods, can now be produced**. This increases the **future SOL and alleviates the problem of scarcity** since more of man's unlimited wants can be satisfied.

Evaluation

However, with economic growth, expectations may increase and even greater levels of consumption may be desired (especially for luxury goods). More wants may also be desired, for example from desiring only to own 1 car to desiring owning 1 car for family rides and another sports car for thrills. This exacerbates the problem of scarcity.

Additionally, **regardless of how high an economy's PPC may be or how much potential growth is experienced, there will always be combinations of goods and services that exist outside the PPC**, such as point C in Fig 2. This illustrates the **persistent problem of scarcity, where the unlimited human wants always exceed the limited amount of available resources.** Hence, the **problem of scarcity can never be solved as unlimited human wants are never fully satisfied.** When existing wants are satisfied, we will always have new, unattainable wants.

Furthermore, economic growth can lead to the depletion of resources. Examples of this phenomenon include overfishing, using up oil reserves and destruction of ecological capital like forests. This could **lead to even fewer resources in the future and hence an inward shift of the PPC**. Therefore, economic growth can in fact further compound the problem of scarcity, as more wants become unattainable.

Finally, while economic growth may be desirable in terms of increasing the material SOL by increasing goods and services available for consumption, there can be detrimental effects to the non-material standard of living such as a fall in leisure time and air pollution, which cannot be illustrated using the PPC. This further suggests that the unlimited human wants cannot be satisfied through economic growth, and although the problem of scarcity may be alleviated, it cannot be eliminated.

2. Explain the AD-AS Model and how equilibrium national income is achieved.

Aggregate demand (AD) refers to the **total quantity demanded of final goods and services** produced by a country at **each and every general price level (GPL)**. It is represented by the AD curve, and comprises of the following components as represented by this formula: $AD = C + I + G + (X-M)$ where

C = Households' expenditures on final goods and services
I = Investment spending by firms on capital goods
G = Government expenditure on final goods and services

X = Total export revenue   ⎤ Together, X-M makes up
M = Total import expenditure ⎦ net exports

Aggregate supply (AS) refers to the **total quantity of final goods and services** producers are willing and able to offer for sale at **each and every GPL in a given time period**. It is represented by the AS curve, which describes the relationship between price levels and the amount of output that firms are willing to produce. It comprises of the short-run aggregate supply (SRAS), which is the horizontal part of the AS curve, and long-run aggregate supply (LRAS), which is the vertical portion of the AS curve, as well as an intermediate range. The SRAS is mainly influenced by **unit costs of production (COP)** while the LRAS is influenced by the **quality and quantity of resources in the economy, as well as the state of technology.** General Price Level (GPL) refers to the average price of all final goods and services produced in an economy in a given time period.

The AD-AS model **shows the relationship between national output and the GPL** in the economy based on changes in AD and AS. Since the value of output produced by the economy, indicated by real Gross Domestic Product (real GDP), is also the amount of national income, the national income equilibrium is therefore a level of national income that is stable with no tendency to change and occurs where AD = AS.

GPL

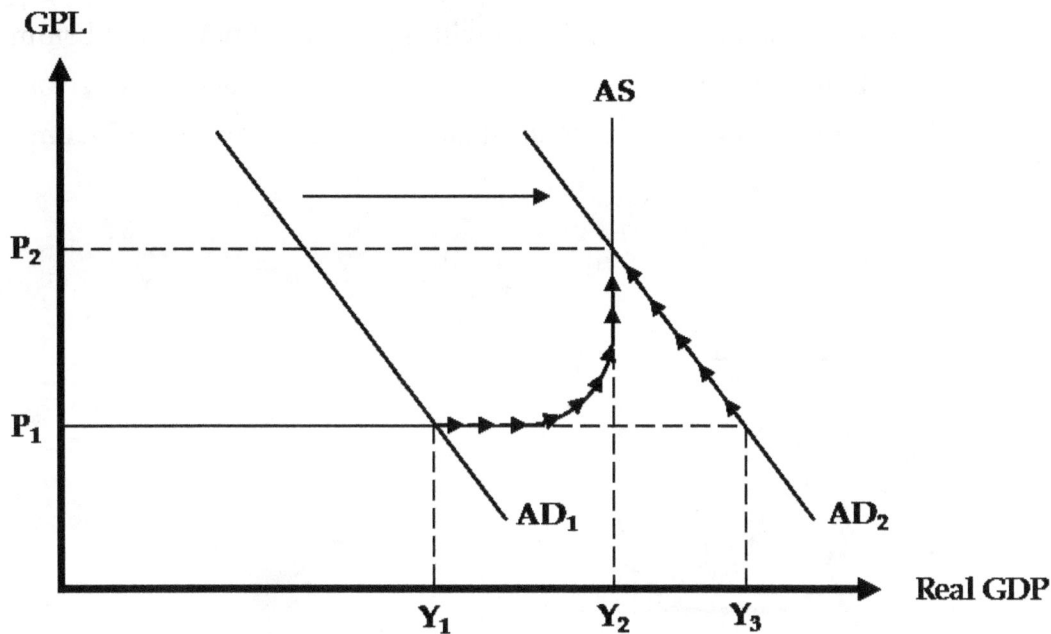

Fig 1: Adjustment Process with Increasing AD

An economy initially produces at the equilibrium Y_1, where $AD_1 = AS$. At this point, the total quantity demanded for final goods and services in the economy equals to the total quantity supplied at the level of Y_1. All the planned expenditure on goods and services is met by corresponding production of these goods and services, and firms therefore **do not need to increase or decrease production.** Hence, the economy is said to be in equilibrium.

Suppose there is now an increase in AD as represented by the rightward shift in AD from AD_1 to AD_2. At initial general price levels of P_0, quantity demanded exceeds quantity supplied by Y_1Y_3. This **exerts an upward pressure on prices** as consumers, firms, the government and foreigners who are unable to obtain the goods will start bidding up prices to compete for limited amount of goods. As price levels rise, the quantity demanded for goods and services produced by the economy will fall due to the wealth effect, interest rate effect and international substitution effect (movement along AD) from Y_3 to Y_2. For example, as price levels rise, the real value of wealth will fall, as households cannot purchase as much goods and services now with the same amount of wealth. This will result in a fall in consumption and hence a fall in quantity demanded for final goods and services. As price levels rise, **producers are also incentivized to produce more** since their profit margins have increased. Hence, planned output will rise while planned expenditure will fall until the new equilibrium is reached at AD = AS at P_2 and output of Y_2, where firms do not increase nor decrease production. **National income has therefore increased and reached a new equilibrium**.

GPL

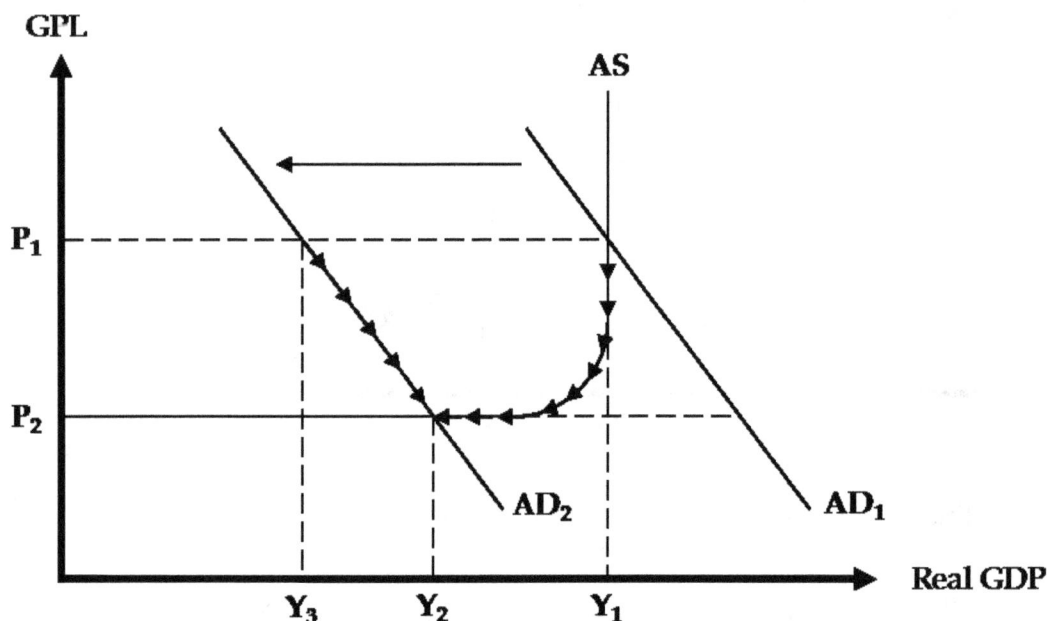

Fig 2: Adjustment Process with Decreasing AD

Conversely, suppose there is now a decrease in AD as represented by the leftward shift in AD from AD_1 to AD_2 in Fig 2. At initial general price levels of P_1, total quantity supplied exceeds total quantity demanded by Y_1Y_3. This exerts a downward pressure on prices as producers who are unable to clear their stocks will lower their selling price in order to do so competitively. As price levels fall, producers are incentivized to produce less as their profit margins have decreased, while the total quantity demanded for goods and services produced by the economy will rise due to the wealth effect, interest rate effect and international substitution effect (movement along AD) from Y_3 to Y_2. For example, as price levels fall, the real value of wealth will rise, as households can now purchase more goods and services now with the same amount of wealth. This will result in an increase in consumption and hence an increase in total quantity demanded for final goods and services. Therefore, following a fall in the AD, planned output will fall while planned expenditure will rise until the new equilibrium is reached at AD_2 = AS at P_2 and output of Y_2, where firms do not increase nor decrease production. National income has therefore decreased and reached a new equilibrium.

Similar to demand and supply in microeconomics, the AD and AS curves intersect to give the equilibrium general price level and output produced by the economy, which is also equal to the real GDP or national income.

3. Explain why the aggregate demand is downward sloping.

The aggregate demand (AD) curve is downwards sloping. There is an inverse relationship between the total quantity demanded and the general price level (GPL) of goods and services in the economy. **As the GPL falls, quantity demanded increases.** This can be explained via 3 effects: The **wealth effect, the interest rate effect and the international substitution effect.**

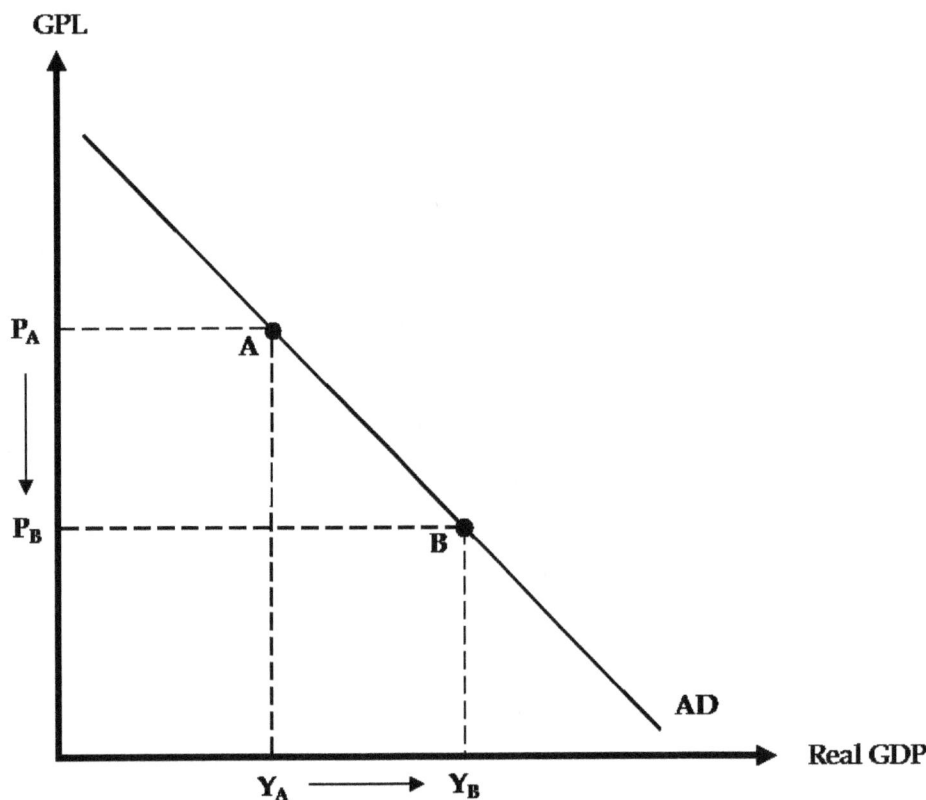

Fig 1: Downward Sloping AD

The Wealth Effect

As **GPL falls** from P_A to P_B, the **real value of wealth increases** because households are now **able to buy more with their current amount of wealth**, as goods and services are now cheaper. As purchasing power increases, the **total quantity demanded of final goods and services in the economy increases** from Y_A to Y_B.

For example, a **fall in GPL** in the economy corresponds with **a fall in prices of certain goods and services** that Mr Tan usually purchases from the supermarket. In the past,

Mr Tan's savings of $4000 could only buy 200 chicken wings. However, because prices have fallen, including the prices of chicken wings, **Mr Tan's savings of $4000 can now buy more chicken wings**. Hence, Mr Tan's purchasing power rises and he demands more chicken wings than before. In an entire economy, millions of people like Mr Tan demanding more goods and services because of an **increase in real value of wealth** therefore results in an increase in the total quantity demanded of goods and services. This leads to a downward sloping AD curve.

The Interest Rate Effect

As **GPL falls** from P_A to P_B, people **require less money to make purchases** on goods and services and this leads to a fall in the demand for money. As the demand for money falls, more households are willing and able to save up in Banks in the form of savings deposits. This increases the supply of loanable funds, resulting in a downward pressure on interest rates. Due to the decrease in interest rates, **consumption that is interest rate sensitive such as those for big ticket items like cars as well as investments (firms' purchase of capital goods) will increase**, leading to an increase in quantity demanded from Y_A to Y_B.

The International Substitution Effect

As **GPL falls** from P_A to P_B, **imports become relatively more expensive compared to domestically produced goods and services**. As such, consumers will reduce **demand for imports and switch to domestically produced goods and services**, assuming that the domestically produced goods and services are substitutes to imports. Hence, **quantity demanded for domestically produced goods and services will increase. At the same time, with the fall in GPL, prices of exports become cheaper relative to the prices of foreign-produced goods and services**, hence **quantity demanded for exports will increase.** Therefore, quantity demanded for goods and services produced by the economy will increase from Y_A to Y_B.

4. **Explain the ranges of the aggregate supply curve.**

GPL

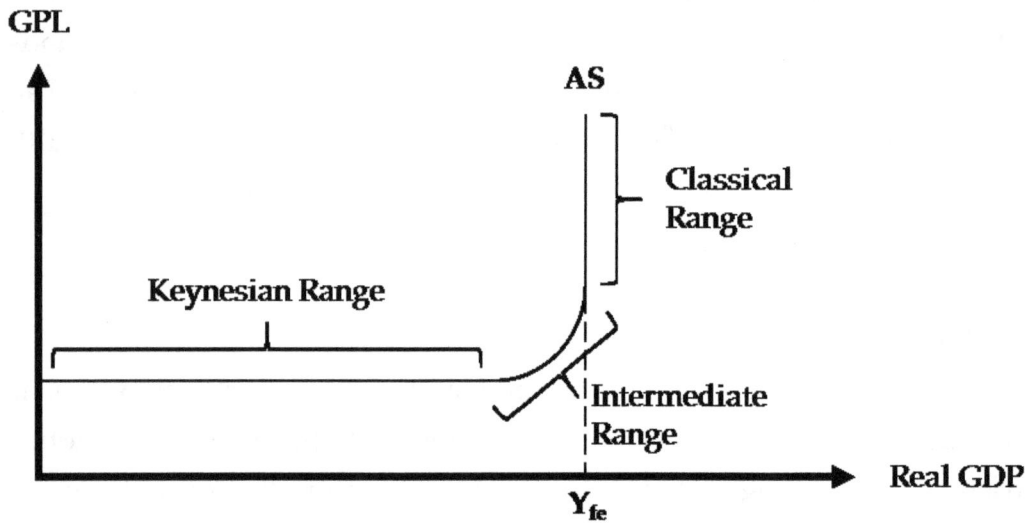

Fig 1: Ranges of AS Curve

The aggregate supply (AS) is made up of 3 ranges; the **Keynesian**, the **Intermediate** and the **Classical** ranges.

The Keynesian Range

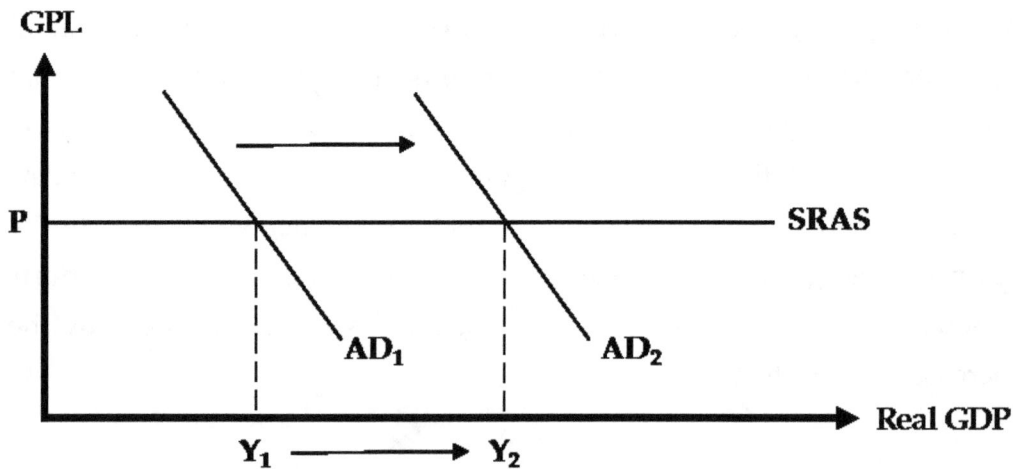

Fig 2: Keynesian Range

The Keynesian range of the AS curve represents the short-run aggregate supply (SRAS). On the Keynesian range, the economy is experiencing a large degree of unemployment as it is **operating far below its productive capacity**. In this range, the economy is said to have significant spare capacity as **factors of production are mostly unutilized.** As such, any increase in aggregate demand (AD), from AD_1 to AD_2 in Fig 2, and total output, from Y_1 to Y_2, will not cause an increase in the prices of factors of production, since there are still a lot of resources unutilised and therefore **no need for firms to compete for resources.** Even though firms begin to hire more people, **wages do not increase as there is a huge surplus of idle workers.** As prices of factors of production remain the same, unit cost of production (COP) remains the same and hence general price level (GPL) stays constant at P in Fig 2 even as real GDP increases in the Keynesian range.

Even if AD falls from AD_2 to AD_1 in Fig 2, GPL remains the same. Although this leads to greater levels of unemployment, due to factors such as fixed wage contracts, resistance from trade unions and minimum wage laws, **wages will not fall even though the surplus of workers has increased.** Since the unit COP does not fall, GPL also stays constant at P as real GDP falls by a large extent from Y_2 to Y_1.

The Intermediate Range

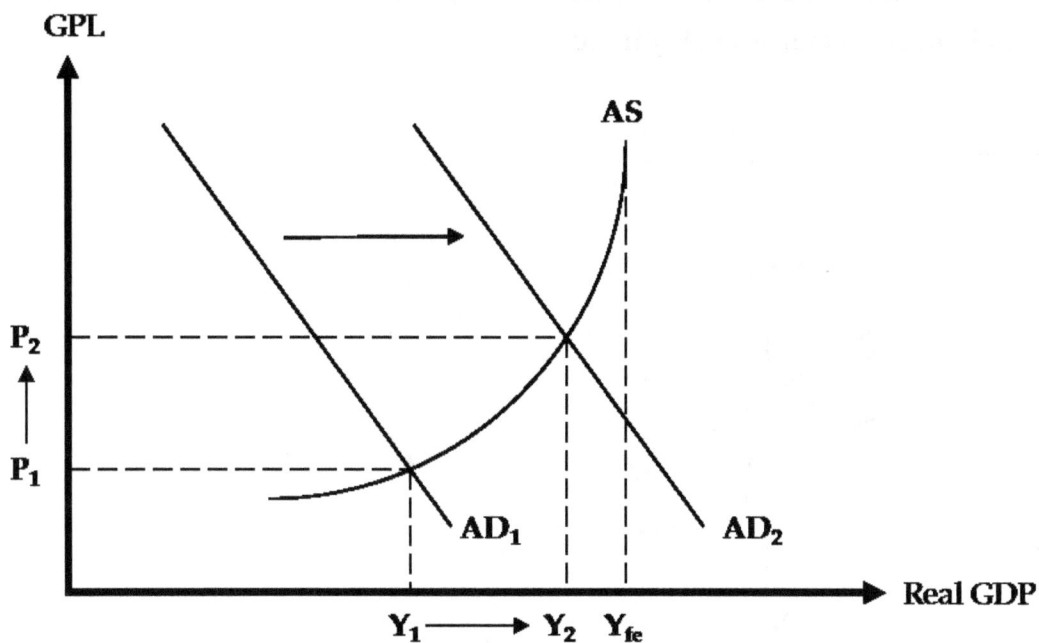

Fig 3: Intermediate Range

The intermediate range lies between the Keynesian range and the classical range. In the intermediate range, **firms can increase output, but do so at the expense of incurring**

17

higher unit COP. This is due to the fact that there is lesser spare capacity in the economy as most resources have already been employed. Therefore, as firms increase production, **firms bid up prices to compete for increasingly scarce factors of production**. Hence, unit COP will rise and firms will eventually pass on these higher costs to consumers in the form of higher prices. GPL increases from P_1 to P_2 as real GDP increases from Y_1 to Y_2 as shown in the Fig 3.

For example, an economy that has recovered from a recession now has relatively lower unemployment rate at Y_2 as compared to Y_1 before. This means that there are much **fewer workers that are unemployed** and **firms may have to compete for workers that are mostly already employed.** This competition **gives workers the opportunity to demand higher wages while firms are also willing to offer higher wages to obtain these workers** to increase production. Hence, unit labour costs and unit COP increase. The increase in the unit COP will eventually lead to higher prices as firms seek to pass on the higher costs to consumers. This can be achieved since AD is increasing. The increase in GPL also indicates the higher prices that firms will need to receive in order to produce more since unit COP have increased. Hence, in the intermediate range, **both the GPL and total output increase as AD increases.**

The Classical Range

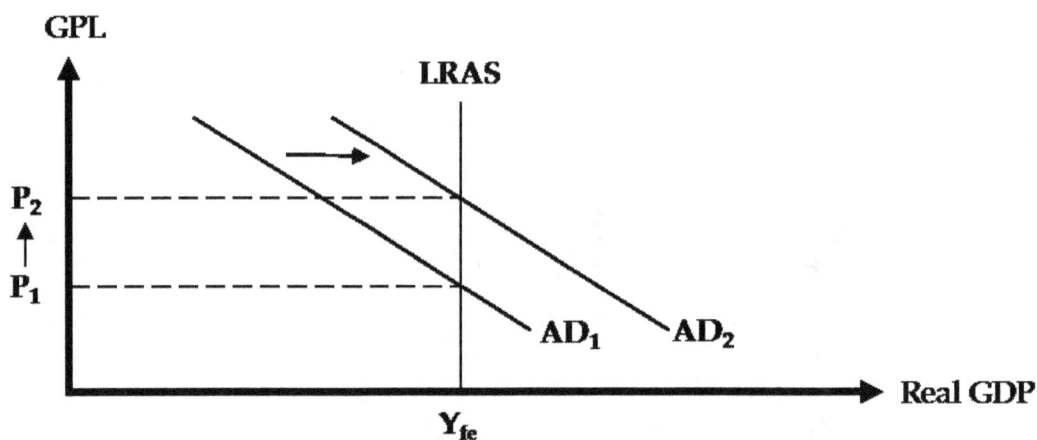

Fig 4: Classical Range

The classical range of the AS curve represents the long-run aggregate supply (LRAS). On the classical range, **the economy is at full employment.** All available factors of production, whether land, labour, capital or entrepreneurship, are being utilised. The

18

full employment level of output is also said to correspond with the natural rate of unemployment - where there is zero cyclical unemployment, but frictional and structural unemployment can still be present. The economy is **unable to further increase real output** because there are **no more available factors of production.** Hence, any further increase in AD, such as that from AD_1 to AD_2 in Fig 4, only cause increased competition between firms for already employed factors of production, resulting in steeply rising factor prices and increase in GPL from P_1 to P_2 but **constant real GDP at Y_{fe}.**

For example, as government spending on construction projects increase, AD increases. Construction firms will now have to compete with other firms, such as firms from the shipping industry, for workers. The construction firms would have to offer the shipyard workers **higher wages in order to attract them.** Furthermore, existing workers in the shipyard firms can demand pay raises from their existing employer and due to the shortage of workers, these firms will be more amenable to such demands. As such, **wages will rise across the economy, resulting in an increase in unit COP and subsequently a rise in GPL from P_1 to P_2.** However, because all factors of production have already been used up, no matter how workers switch from one job to another between firms, the total output of the economy remains the same at Y_{fe}. The increased production in the construction sector occurs as resources are diverted from other sectors, reducing production in these other sectors. Hence, the **increase in GPL is not accompanied by any increase in real output. At this range, increasing AD only results in high rates of inflation and without actual economic growth.**

Any point of output on the classical range represents full employment Y_{fe}), meaning there is no cyclical unemployment although other forms of unemployment (structural, frictional) may still be present. These forms of unemployment cannot be illustrated on an AD-AS diagram. Conversely, any point of output to the left of the classical range represents the presence of cyclical unemployment. Note that at this point there is still a presence of frictional and structural unemployment. Some amount of frictional and structural unemployment is normal and in fact inevitable for a vibrant and growing economy. Hence, when the economy is on the classical range, it experiences a "natural rate" of unemployment.

5. Explain the significance of the different ranges of the aggregate supply.

Knowing the different ranges of the AS will give us greater insight into the performance and state of the economy. Based on whether the AD curve intersects the AS curve at the Keynesian, Intermediate or Classical range, one can ascertain whether or not the economy may soon be overheating or whether resources are significantly unutilised.

Knowing the state of the economy then allows for the government to determine the appropriate macroeconomic policies to enact, based on the effects that demand-management policies have on AD and supply-side policies on AS. It also allows the Government to gauge the effectiveness of these policies.

On the Keynesian Range

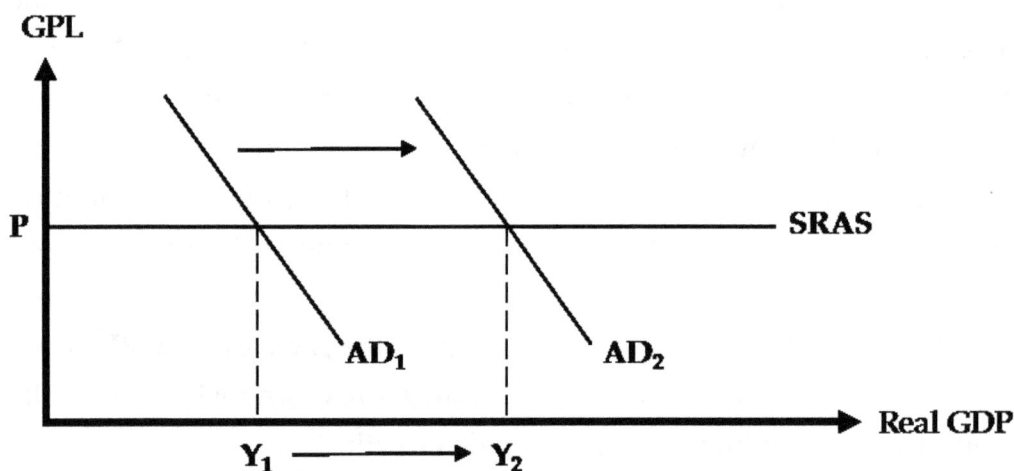

Fig 1: Keynesian Range

If the economy is operating on the Keynesian range, this means that there is a large degree of unemployment and therefore a lot of spare capacity. When demand-management policies such as expansionary fiscal and monetary policies aggressively stimulate AD, AD is raised from AD_1 to AD_2 in Fig 1. Due to abundance of spare capacity, a rise in AD need not lead to a rise in general price levels (GPL). As GPL stays constant at P, the multiple rounds of induced consumption, arising from the initial autonomous increase in AD, can occur to the fullest extent. This is because the increase in households' incomes is not mitigated by erosion in purchasing power arising from inflation and falling real value of money. Hence the economy experiences the full

20

multiplier effect, with real GDP increasing by a multiplied amount from Y_1 to Y_2, allowing for non-inflationary economic growth and making demand-management policies most effective in the Keynesian range. In order to increase production, firms will have to increase the derived demand for factors of production such as labour. This increases the quantity of labour hired, hence decreasing cyclical unemployment.

On the Intermediate Range

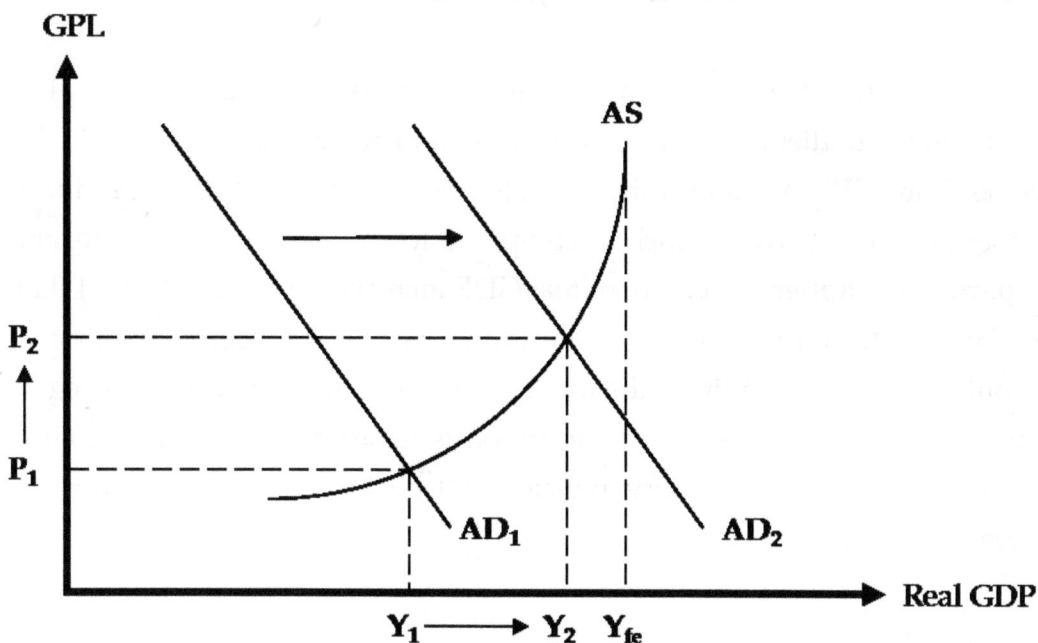

Fig 2: Intermediate Range

If the economy is operating on the intermediate range, governments will have to **carefully weigh the costs and benefits of policies that they implement** to achieve their goals. The intermediate range of the AS is a good example of how conflicts in macro goals can arise. In pursuing economic growth, inflation will begin to occur. Conversely, reducing inflation would lead to slower economic growth.

If the government wishes to reduce inflation, implementing policies that reduce AD in order to achieve a lower GPL will also lead to increased unemployment and negative (or slowdown in) growth. As AD falls from AD_2 to AD_1, GPL falls from P_2 to P_1, but real GDP also falls from Y_2 to Y_1.

On the other hand, if the government wishes to increase employment, expansionary fiscal or monetary policies will increase AD from AD_1 to AD_2 and lead to greater economic growth with real GDP increasing from Y_1 to Y_2, as well as decreased cyclical unemployment, but also an increase in GPL from P_1 to P_2 and thus a higher rate of inflation.

On the intermediate range, **short-run supply-side policies will be ideal** as an increase in the SRAS will lead to **both increases in employment as well as a fall in GPL.**

The intermediate range also results in a smaller multiplier effect. On the intermediate range, there is a supply bottleneck and some competition for resources. Hence, GPL begins to increase. Since GPL increases, this will deter consumption and hence, induced consumption does not increase by as much as compared to at the Keynesian range, and there is only a **partial multiplier effect** where real GDP increases by a lesser extent than expected. For example, even if the size of the multiplier is 5, at the intermediate range real GDP may only increase by 2.5 times the amount of the initial increase in aggregate expenditure, as the induced increase in consumption is lesser due to the rising GPL. Hence, expansionary fiscal and monetary policies will be **less effective** in boosting economic growth on this range.

On the Classical Range

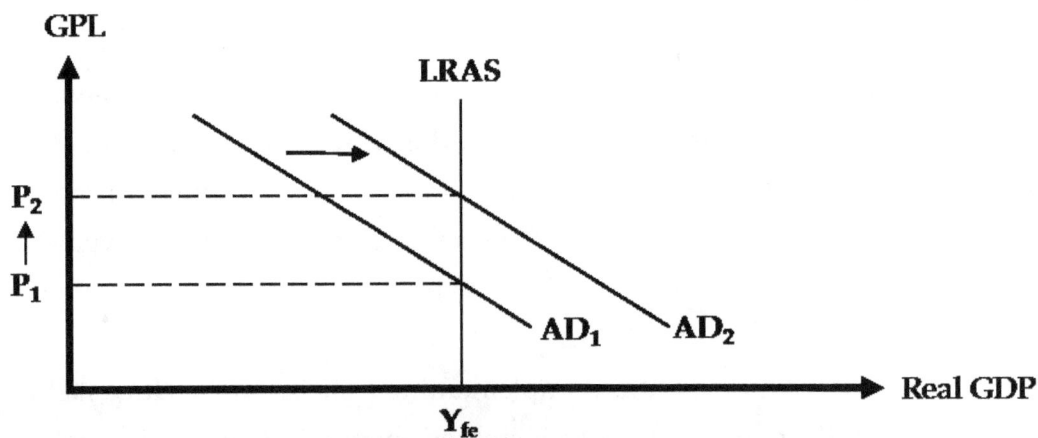

Fig 3: Classical Range

If the economy is operating on the classical range, the economy is likely to be overheating. Demand management policies **will not lead to any increase in real GDP.**

It will **only lead to high rates of inflation** due to a lack of spare capacity and producers aggressively bidding up prices for severely scarce factors of production. As AD increases from AD_1 to AD_2, there is no increase in real GDP but GPL has increased from P_1 to P_2. There is zero multiplier effect at this range as any increase in AD does not result in an increase in real GDP.

On this range, governments **can actively pursue contractionary fiscal and monetary policies to reduce the problem of inflation without sacrificing economic growth and increasing unemployment.** This is due to the fact that on the classical range, any decrease in AD will not lead to a decrease in real GDP and employment. However, in doing so, governments run the risk of underestimating the contractionary effects of their policies and may instead end up triggering a recession due to an over-contraction of the economy.

Governments can also choose to pursue long-run supply-side policies in order to expand productive capacity, resulting in a rightward shift in the AS curve. Doing so will result in potential growth, create more spare capacity, ease demand-pull inflationary pressures and allow for greater actual growth via more increase in AD.

6. Explain what determines actual and potential growth.

Actual growth refers to the **annual percentage increase in national output actually produced.** It can be caused by an increase in any of the components of Aggregate Demand (AD), namely consumption (C), investments (I), government expenditure (G) or net exports (X-M), ceteris paribus. It can also result from an increase in the short-run aggregate supply (SRAS) of the economy.

Actual Growth with Increasing AD

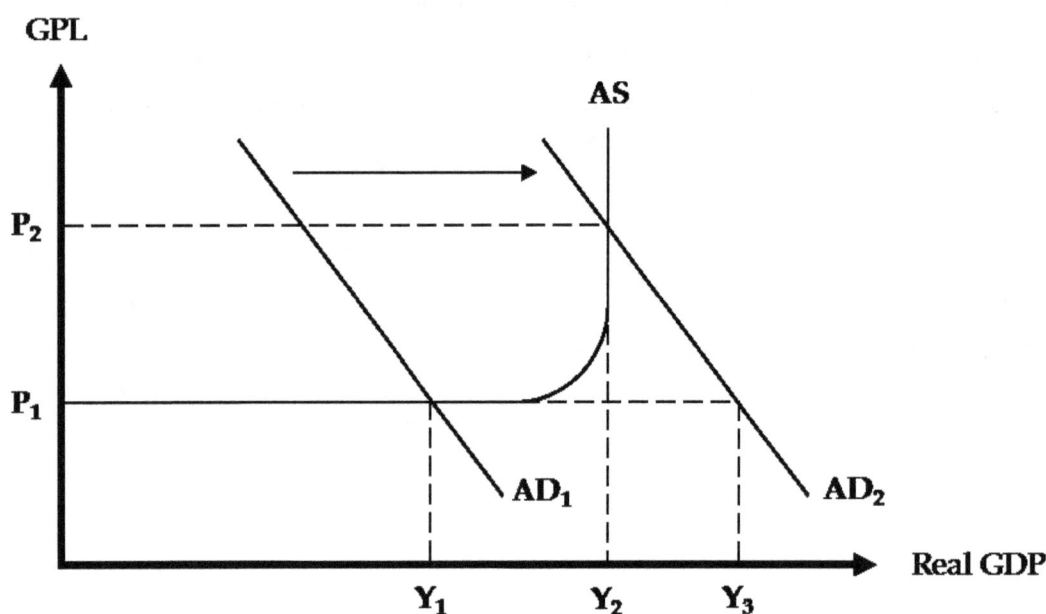

Fig 1: Actual Growth with Increasing AD

❖ **Economic Growth of Trading Partners**

Suppose there is strong economic growth overseas. As incomes of foreigners increase, this can lead to increasing demand for exports, assuming they are normal goods. Hence export revenue (X) increases, and assuming import expenditure (M) remains constant, this will result in an increase in the net exports (X-M), thereby increasing AD from AD_1 to AD_2. At initial general price level (GPL) of P_1, quantity demanded exceeds quantity supplied by Y_3Y_1. This **exerts an upward pressure on prices** as consumers, firms, government and foreigners who are unable to obtain the goods will start bidding up prices. As price levels increase, the quantity demanded for goods and services produced by the economy will fall from Y_3 to Y_2, due to the wealth, interest rate and international substitution effects. As price levels increase, **producers are incentivized to produce more** since their profit margins have increased, increasing quantity supplied from Y_1 to Y_2. Hence, planned output will increase while planned expenditure will fall until the new equilibrium is reached at $AD_2 = AS$ at P_2 and output of Y_2. Thus, there is actual growth with increase in real GDP from Y_1 to Y_2.

❖ **Expectations**

AD may also increase due to **optimistic expectations of the future state of the economy**. With expectations of continued growth in incomes and job stability, there will be strong consumer and business confidence, and consumers will **be more willing to spend,** including on big-ticket items like cars, raising C. Both domestic and foreign firms expect higher rates of return on investments, thereby increasing their level of investments and raising I. As C and I are components of AD, AD will increase, ceteris paribus. Conversely, with lower consumer and business confidence, the economy is likely to experience an economic slowdown with a slower rate of actual growth or even a recession.

Furthermore, **expectations of future prices** can also affect consumption and hence AD. If households **expect prices to increase** in the future, they will **spend more today** especially on non-perishable products in order to avoid paying higher prices in the future, leading to an **increase in C and hence AD**. Conversely, if **prices are expected to fall** in the future, consumers will **spend less in the current time period** and await the fall in prices before spending. This dampens AD and slows down economic growth.

❖ **Government Policies**

Government policies can affect C and I, thereby influencing AD. A cut in the **personal income taxes** levied by the government **increases the disposable income** of households. In addition, government spending in the form of **transfer payments** will also **increase the disposable income of households**. Households will therefore experience an increase in purchasing power, resulting in an increase in C hence increasing AD. Furthermore, the government can **reduce corporate tax rates**. This will increase after tax profits and hence expected rate of return on investments. Therefore, I will increase hence increasing AD.

The government can also directly increase AD through an increase in G. This can be achieved by **increasing government consumption,** for example, by **hiring more workers to work in the civil service**, or by **increasing the bonuses of existing civil servants**. In addition, the government can also undertake **more public works projects**. This will mean purchasing more contractor services, thereby increasing G and hence increasing AD.

❖ **Protectionism**

Protectionism is a policy of favouring domestic industries over foreign competition. For example, the Government may impose tariffs, an indirect tax on imports. This will increase the prices of imports, causing households to switch from imports to domestically produced goods and services. Hence M falls, causing X-M to increase, increasing the AD.

Should other countries remove or reduce tariffs on this country's exports, this will help increase the price competitiveness of exports, increasing quantity demanded for exports and X. Assuming M remains the same, net exports (X-M) will increase, leading to an increase in AD.

❖ **The Multiplier**

The extent of actual growth will also be determined by the size of the multiplier (K). The multiplier effect occurs when an **increase in autonomous spending** produces an **increase in national income greater than the initial amount of increase in spending.** The formula for the change in national income is equal to k x (change in aggregate expenditure). The larger the value of the multiplier, the greater the increase in national output given an initial increase in consumption, investments, government expenditure or net exports.

The size of k is in turn determined by:

$$k = \frac{1}{1 - MPC} = \frac{1}{MPW} = \frac{1}{MPM + MPT + MPS} = \frac{Change\ in\ GDP}{Change\ in\ Autonomous\ Spending}$$

where MPC is the marginal propensity to consume, MPW is the marginal propensity to withdraw, MPM is the marginal propensity to import, MPT is the marginal propensity to tax, MPS is marginal propensity to save. The marginal propensity of each function is defined as the proportion of additional income used for that function e.g. if MPC = 0.8, it means that 80% of any additional income to all households is used for consumption.

For example, if the size of k = 5, an initial increase in government spending of $1 billion will lead to an increase in national income of $5 billion. Hence, the larger the value of k, the more actual growth is achieved with an increase in initial government spending.

Actual Growth with Increasing SRAS

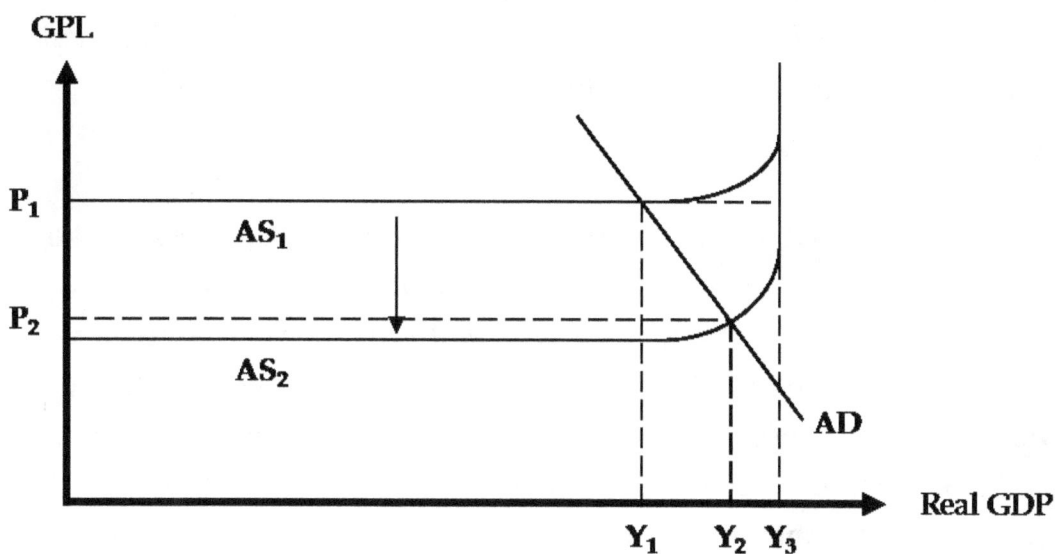

Fig 2: Actual Growth with Increasing SRAS

Actual growth can also be brought about by **an increase in the SRAS**. That is usually caused by a fall in the unit costs of production (COP). As **COP falls** due to a fall in prices of factor inputs such as a fall in wages, SRAS increases from AS_1 to AS_2 in Fig 2. Firms are hence willing and able **to produce more** output at each GPL. At the existing GPL of P_1, actual output exceeds total quantity demanded by Y_3Y_1. This surplus exerts a downward pressure on prices, as producers attempt to clear their excess stocks, resulting in a fall in GPL from P_1 to P_2. As the GPL falls, total quantity demanded increases from Y_1 to Y_2 as a result of the wealth, interest rate and international substitution effects, while actual output falls from Y_3 to Y_2, as the profit incentive to produce is reduced, resulting in a new equilibrium at P_2, Y_2. Therefore, **real GDP increases** from Y_1 to Y_2 and actual growth occurs.

❖ **Prices of Inputs**

A fall in prices of inputs will increase SRAS. As prices of inputs fall, unit COP will fall, resulting in firms being willing and able to produce more at each and every GPL, hence increasing SRAS. For example, oil is an essential factor of production for almost every industry. The current situation of falling oil prices in 2015 will result in a fall in unit COP world-wide, resulting in an increase in SRAS for most economies.

Government policies may involve subsidies to firms **reduce firms' unit COP** and hence increase SRAS. Governments may do this for **critical raw materials that firms across various sectors of the economy require**. For example, the Malaysian and Indonesian governments subsidize fuel in order to lower the unit COP.

❖ **Unit Labour Costs**

Labour productivity is defined as the **amount of output produced per worker hour. Unit labour cost** (ULC) measures the **average cost of labour per unit of output**. If wage increases more than labour productivity does, ULC will increase. Conversely, if wage increases less than labour productivity does, ULC falls. Hence, ULC is **affected by wages of workers** and the **productivity of workers**. Wages may be significantly influenced by the **presence of strong trade unions** in a country, while productivity of workers is affected by **the amount of education and training** undergone by these workers. It is also affected by the amount of capital goods and level of technology available. As ULC falls, unit COP also falls, **resulting in an increase in SRAS.**

❖ **Beneficial Supply Shocks**

Beneficial supply shocks such as an unexpectedly good weather for the agricultural economy could increase the amount of available agricultural goods and hence result in an increase in SRAS.

Potential Growth with Increasing LRAS

GPL

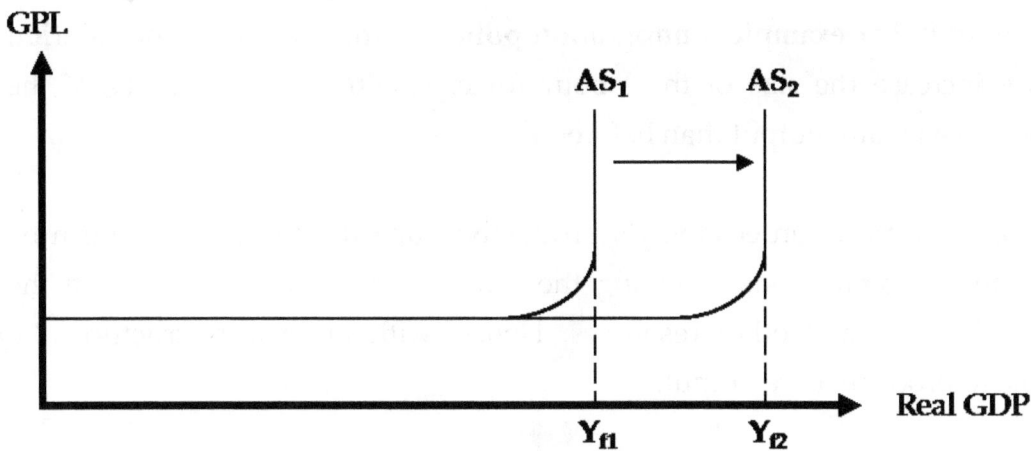

Fig 3: Potential Growth with Increasing LRAS

Potential growth refers to the **increase in the productive capacity** of the economy over time. It can be due to increases in the **quality or quantity of factors of production** i.e. land, labour, capital and entrepreneurship. It can also be a result of advances in the state of technology. These will enable the economy to produce more if it were to use all available resources, thereby increasing the long-run aggregate supply (LRAS) of the economy from AS_1 to AS_2 in Fig 3. Hence, the full employment level of output increases from Y_{f1} to Y_{f2}.

❖ **Increase in Quality of Factors of Production**

As the quality of resources increase, we are able to produce more with the same amount of scarce resources. As the quality of labour increases due to skills training and education, the same amount of labour can yield greater output. Therefore, the productive capacity of the economy increases.

There could also be some upgrading of infrastructure – such as to upgrade the traditional rail network to a high speed one. This is an increase in the quality of capital in an economy, increasing its efficiency and hence the maximum amount of output it can produce.

❖ **Increase in Quantity of Factors of Production**

As the quantity of resources increase, we now have more resources and can hence produce more output. **For example, immigration policies can increase the population size** and hence increase the size of the labour force, resulting in the ability of the economy to produce greater output than before.

Infrastructure also increases an economy's productive capacity. Infrastructure can be considered as huge capital goods, allowing the economy to produce more with the same amount of labour and other resources. Hence, with more infrastructure, the economy is able to produce more output.

❖ **Advancement in Technology**

Technological advancements can give rise to methods of production that yield greater output from fewer inputs. This will increase the amount of output the economy can produce with the same amount of scarce resources. Hence, productive capacity increases and potential growth results.

Evaluation:

Importance of Supply-side Policies

Potential growth heavily depends on supply-side policies that can either increase the quality and quantity of resources or the level of technology in the economy. Subsidies for education, training, research and development and development expenditure on infrastructure all contribute to increasing the economy's LRAS and hence result in potential growth. The development expenditure by the government can also have demand-side effects by increasing G, hence contributing to increasing AD and achieving actual growth.

However, each supply-side policy has its own limitations. For example, policies directed at education and training are long-term policies that are highly dependent on the receptiveness, attitude and aptitude of the recipient receiving the education and training, thus they may be unsuccessful if recipients are resistant to learning new skills or are simply unable to due to lack of sufficient aptitude. Research and development, on the other hand, is a risky venture which may not necessarily result in technological advancements, hence may be unsuccessful in achieving potential growth as well.

Nature of Economy

For actual growth due to increased AD, the source of increased AD and subsequent growth can vary between different economies, based on the nature of each economy. Large economies such as the United States tend to be more consumption driven due to the presence of a large domestic market, with C contributing to a large proportion of Real GDP. Hence, domestic demand is a major driver of actual growth. On the other hand, small economies such as Singapore tend to be export driven due to the smallness of their domestic markets. They depend on a much larger global market, with X being a large proportion their Real GDP. External demand is a major driver of actual growth.

Preference for Actual or Potential Growth

It is largely understood that both actual and potential growth are required in the long run in order to achieve sustainable non-inflationary economic growth, which is a key macroeconomic goal and which will be explored in the next chapter, Chapter 7. Whether or not the government should prioritise achieving actual or potential growth is dependent on the current state of the economy in terms of the amount of spare capacity available. This has been explored in the previous chapter, Chapter 5.

7. **Explain why an economy should pursue both actual and potential growth.**

Economic growth refers to the **increase in an economy's real Gross Domestic Product (GDP), or real national output, over time. Actual growth** refers to the **percentage annual increase in national output actually produced.** In contrast, **potential growth** refers to the **increase in the productive capacity** of the economy over time.

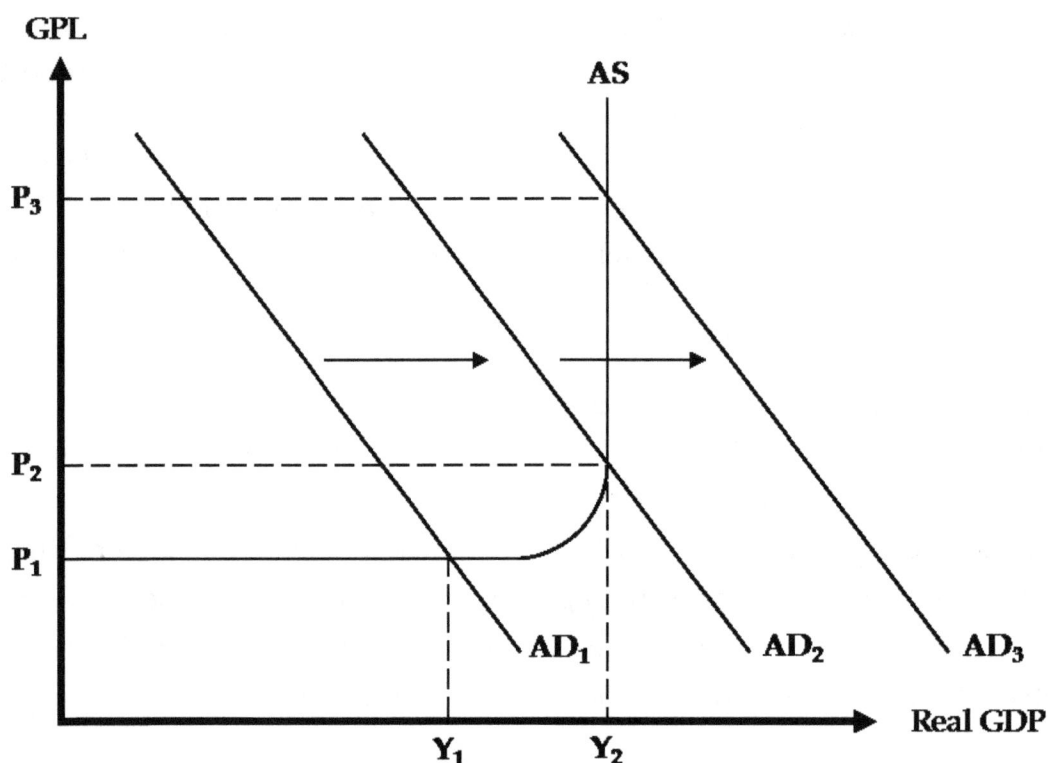

Fig 1: Increasing AD

Actual growth is desirable as **it increases national income** and **decreases unemployment,** resulting in **a higher material standard of living (SOL).** As aggregate demand increases from AD_1 to AD_2 in Fig 1, there is **actual growth** in the economy as **firms increase production to meet the unplanned decrease in stocks and inventories.** Firm' demand for workers increase and hence **more workers are employed** to increase production levels. **Unemployment rate falls and real national output increases from Y_1 to Y_2.** Because of the increase in production, **more goods and services are now available for consumption,** and assuming population remaining constant, thereby resulting in an **increase in the material SOL** for the residents in the economy. It also means that households **earn more income** and hence possess **greater purchasing power**, and are able to enjoy **a greater material SOL.**

With more incomes, households can also **afford more education, healthcare and recreational activities,** thus also **improving the non-material SOL,** which consists of the intangible quality-of-life aspects. Furthermore, Governments can obtain **more tax revenues,** since incomes are increasing and thus income tax revenues would also be increasing. Consumption tax revenues could also increase as more consumption is induced by the rise in incomes. This provides the Government with **greater ability to subsidise or provide merit and public goods, such as housing and parks, which can contribute to greater non-material SOL.**

Furthermore, with actual growth, we are also making **better use of available scarce resources** to produce more goods and services to satisfy our unlimited wants, thereby **alleviating the problem of scarcity** and moving towards achieving **productive efficiency.**

However, **potential growth** is also necessary to ensure **sustainable economic growth,** which means that the real national output can continue to increase over time. If AD continues increasing without a corresponding increase in the productive capacity as seen in Fig 1 with AD increasing from AD_2 to AD_3, **real national output will stagnate** at Y_2. This is because at this point, **the economy is said to be at full employment and there is hence no more spare capacity in the economy to further expand production.** Hence, there can be no economic growth beyond Y_2, national income remains constant and **SOL stagnates.**

Furthermore, if AD continues to increase, **demand-pull inflation** can result as evident from the increase in general price level (GPL) from P_2 to P_3. This is due to the lack of any spare capacity and hence, firms compete among themselves for factors of production, paying higher prices for inputs and ultimately passing this cost on to consumers in charging higher prices. This can in fact adversely affect material SOL as the inflation erodes the purchasing power and real income of households, rendering them less able to purchase and consume as many goods and services as before.

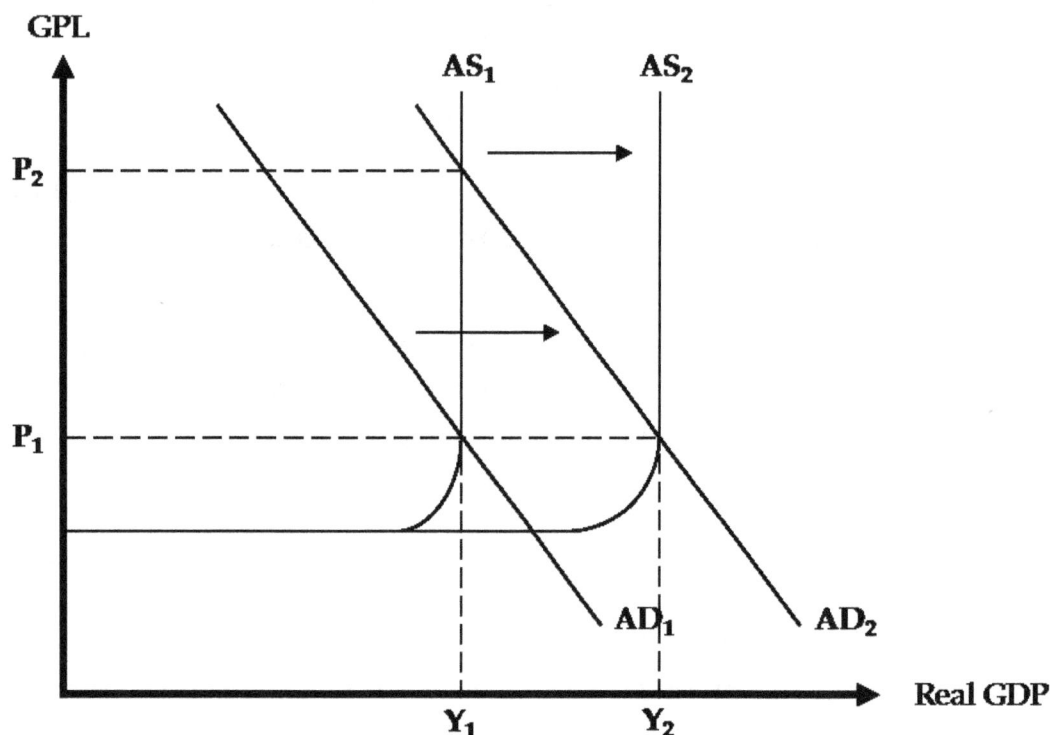

Fig 2: Increasing AD and LRAS

Therefore, potential growth is necessary allow for sustainable economic growth and to prevent a high rate of inflation. Referring to Fig 2, as AD increases from AD_1 to AD_2 on AS_1, there is **zero economic growth as real national output stagnates at Y_1** and **a high inflation rate** as GPL increases from P_1 to P_2.

If there is an increase in the **quality or quantity of resources or technological advancements**, the **productive capacity and LRAS of the economy increases** as represented by a rightward shift in AS curve from AS_1 to AS_2, therefore achieving potential growth. Now, real national output can increase to Y_2 and furthermore, **inflation is avoided** as GPL remains at P_1.

However, potential growth on its own is not enough to ensure sustainable economic growth. If an economy experiences potential growth without actual growth, it means that the economy's potential, while expanding, is not realised. Resources are even more under-utilized and unemployment may have increased. Without actual growth, real national income has not increased and material SOL has not improved. Therefore, it must be recognized that both **actual and potential growth needs to be achieved with**

AD and AS increasing in tandem in order to ensure that the economy achieves sustainable non-inflationary economic growth.

Evaluation

Material SOL is characterised by the amount of goods and services available for consumption by the residents in an economy. As such, sustainable non-inflationary economic growth contributes heavily to increasing material SOL because it increases the amount of goods and services available for consumption with minimal erosion of purchasing power arising from inflation. Non-material SOL, characterised by the qualitative aspects of life, can also be improved as more healthcare and education can also be produced and consumed.

However, material SOL may not necessarily improve if there is high income inequality. The higher incomes may be earned mainly by the already high income groups in the economy, while the masses may not actually enjoy much increase in incomes. As a result, even while there could be higher real GDP per capita (Real GDP/Total Population) indicating that the average person in the economy may be earning higher incomes, in reality the distribution of the incomes are so uneven that the masses actually do not experience higher incomes and therefore do not experience an increase in material SOL.

Furthermore, economic growth may arise at the detriment of other aspects of non-material SOL. For example, economic growth may call for a higher rate of industrialisation, resulting in increased number of factories and amount of energy consumption, which in turn results in greater amount of air and water pollution, not only damaging the environment but also generating negative externalities, through possibly causing health problems to residents in the vicinity and lowering their non-material SOL. Increased workload from economic growth can also result in increased stress and reduced leisure time as workers work longer hours, lowering their non-material SOL.

8. Explain what determines the level of investment.

Investments refer to expenditure by firms to acquire new capital goods (man-made goods that can be used to produce other goods) like buildings and large machinery. Investments can come in the form of **foreign direct investments (FDI), domestic fixed capital formation** and in a more general sense, investments can also include **expenditure on the improvement of human capital.**

Whether a firm invests or not is dependent on two main factors, **the Marginal Efficiency of Investment (MEI)** and the **interest rate (i/r)**. Firms are **profit driven** and their decision to commit to an additional unit of investment is based on whether or not the investment will be profitable. Hence, firms will invest if the expected rate of return, or MEI, exceeds the prevailing i/r.

The MEI **is the expected rate of return** for every additional unit of investment. The MEI curve is the demand for investments and shows the quantity of investments demanded at every i/r.

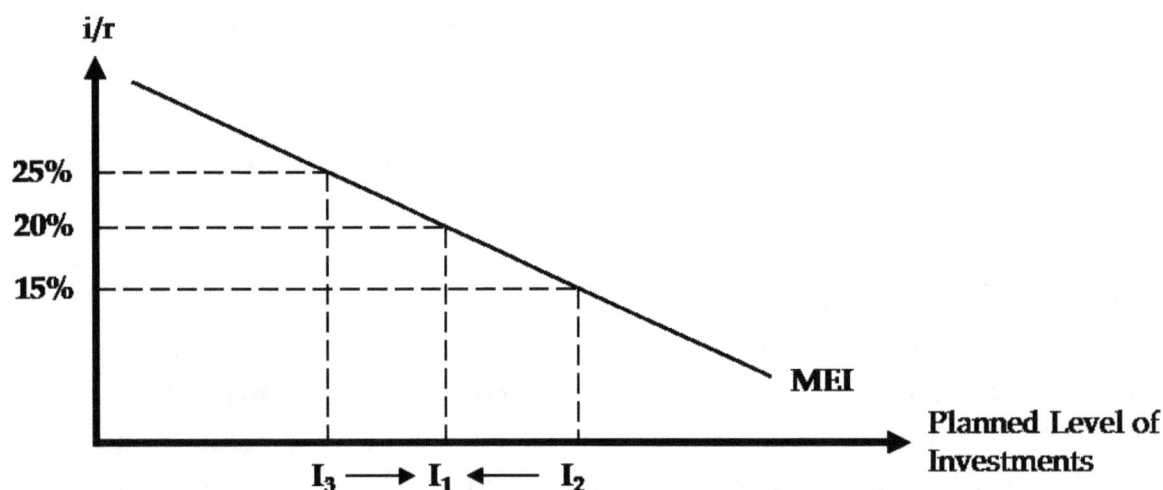

Fig 1: Marginal Efficiency of Investment

The firm has to **weigh the benefits against the costs** of each additional unit of investment. Referring to Fig 1, assuming the current interest rate to be at 20%, a firm should not undertake investments that yield an MEI of less than 20%, as the interest costs it incurs from borrowing from the bank will be more than the expected rate of return from the project, and hence the project is unprofitable. Therefore the firm will only invest up to I_1, instead of up to I_2 which would be the case if the i/r was 15%. If the firm were to use its own funds instead of borrowing, opportunity costs would be incurred and hence, it would be better off **keeping it in the bank to earn the prevailing 20% i/r**, which would be **higher than the expected rate of return at levels of investments beyond I_1.**

On the other hand, if it only invests I_3, it would not be maximizing profits as it is **still profitable for additional units of investments to be undertaken.** The **expected rate of return exceeds the cost of funds for investments**. The firm would **therefore earn more profits by increasing their level of investment up to I_1.**

Therefore, when **MEI > i/r, every additional unit of investments adds to the firm's profits.** When **i/r > MEI, every additional unit causes a loss**. The firm should therefore invest up to the point where **MEI = i/r**, where **the return from the last unit of investment = cost of funds.**

Tip

Interest rates are the cost of borrowing and are also the opportunity cost of funds for investments. Regardless of whether the firm has to borrow to undertake investments, they will still be sensitive to prevailing interest rates. This is due to the fact that opportunity costs can arise from using their own funds in investments since these funds have the next best alternative of being kept in banks to earn interest. Hence, firms will have to weigh the potential rate of return against the prevailing interest rate in order to make investment decisions.

Determinants of the Level of Investments

❖ **Interest Rates**

As i/r represents the cost of funds for investments, a fall in i/r, will now make it **profitable** to undertake certain investment projects that were unprofitable at higher i/r. Hence the level of investments is inversely related to i/r, ceteris paribus.

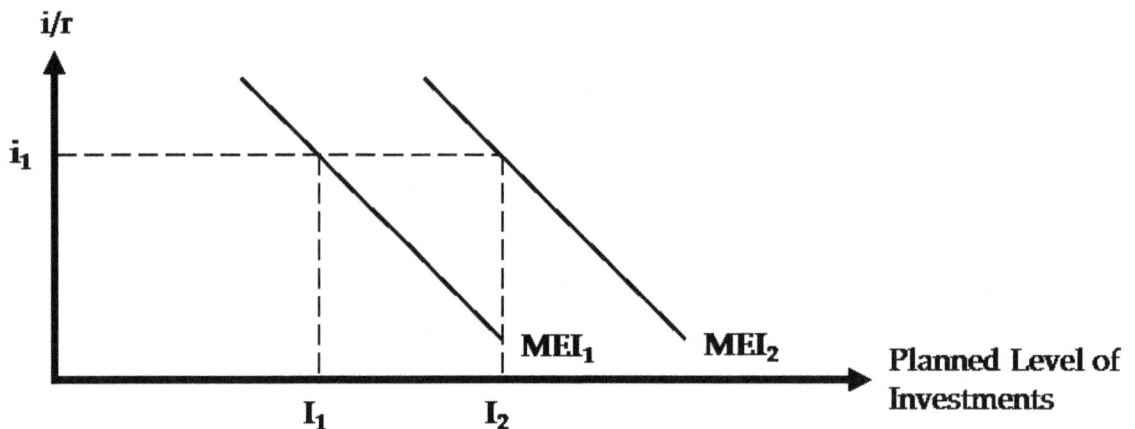

Fig 2: Changing MEI

❖ **Marginal Efficiency of Investment (MEI)**

The MEI is the demand for investments, which is influenced by several factors such as business confidence, political stability, infrastructure, taxes and quality of the workforce. These factors can alter the expected rate of return on investment projects and hence affect the MEI. Factors that cause firms to **revise upwards their expected rate of return** will result in a **rightward shift of the MEI** curve from MEI_1 to MEI_2 in Fig 2, causing an increase in level of investment from I_1 to I_2 at prevailing interest rate i_1. Factors that cause firms to **revise downwards their expected rate of return** will result in a **leftward shift in the MEI** from MEI_2 to MEI_1 in Fig 2, causing a decrease in level of investment from I_2 to I_1 at prevailing interest rate i_1.

❖ **Business Confidence**

Business confidence in the economy, also known as "animal spirits" by Keynes, is a key determinant of the level of investments to be undertaken. **As business sentiments improve, they will likely revise upwards their expectations of future profits. The expected rate of return on investments increases.** Hence, they will be more likely to undertake additional units of investments at each and every prevailing i/r level.

❖ **Political Stability and Industrial Relations**

A **strong and efficient government** can ensure that there is **security and stability** in the country, where **strikes, rioting and crime can be kept to a minimum**. This will result in **greater confidence in the economy** as investments undertaken are more likely to succeed in a stable environment as compared to a volatile one which poses risk to the investments, such as damage to factories and machinery, death of workers, civil unrest etc.

For example, contrast Singapore's strong government and stable political landscape to that of Western European countries. The Singapore government holds a **firm tripartite relationship with trade unions and employers, fostering harmonious collaborative relations.** In Western Europe however, train operator strikes have been common, resulting in the halting of rail transport into and out of Belgium, France and Italy. **These disruptions could pose a risk to the investments undertaken** and hence, ceteris paribus, businesses are more likely to invest in Singapore due to greater stability as compared to a politically unstable economy.

❖ **Government Policies**

Government Policies like **taxes, subsidies or incentives** can increase or decrease the profitability of investments. Soft loans (loans with preferential i/r), technical assistance schemes, reduction in corporate tax, will **reduce costs of production or increase after-tax profits** and hence **increase the expected rate of return on investment.** In Singapore, tax holidays are awarded to pioneer companies while incentives and various assistances are awarded to Small and Medium Enterprises to encourage growth and investments by local companies. Corporate tax has also been kept very low, having been slashed from 40% to 17% over the decades.

❖ **Infrastructure**

Good infrastructure like **effective transport links and a well-developed communications network** can **increase business efficiency thereby lowering costs** of production as well as reducing risk of investments. Effective and reliable transportation **reduce the risk of delays which can result in economic loss** for investors, while a **well-developed communications network increases efficiency as information can be relayed consistently at a moment's notice**. Hence due to **lower risk and lower costs of production, the expected rate of return increases as the quality of infrastructure increases**, resulting in an increase in demand for investments and hence, greater levels of investment at each and every prevailing i/r level.

❖ **Workforce**

As the literacy rate of a country improves, it becomes **easier to train** the workers and they become **more capable of handling complex production processes**. They are usually **more receptive to changes** and also **more productive**. **Labour productivity can hence be more easily increased** through various skills training programmes. This **can lower the unit labour cost and hence the unit cost of production, increasing the expected rate of return** on investments.

In conclusion, the level of investments in an economy is influenced by both the prevailing i/r and the expected rate of return, which is in turn influenced by the various factors discussed above. Government policies can increase the level of investments through both ways; through monetary policy to reduce interest rates or supply side policies such developing a more educated workforce, developing infrastructure, cutting corporate tax rates and promoting political stability.

9. Explain why the demand for investments may be interest-inelastic in Singapore.

Interest elasticity of investments measures the responsiveness of the quantity demanded for investments to a change in the interest rate, ceteris paribus.

The demand for investments is elastic if a change in interest rates results in a more than proportionate change in investments demanded. On the other hand, the demand for investments is inelastic if a change in interest rates results in a less than proportionate decrease in investments demanded.

Investments in Singapore are **mainly by foreign firms in the form of FDI** (70%-80%). These foreign firms, usually Multinational Corporations are likely to **have their own sources of funds** such as borrowings from their local banks or by issuing bonds and shares through stock exchanges where they are listed. Their investment decisions are therefore **unlikely to be affected by Singapore's interest rate**. Hence the demand for investments in Singapore may be interest-inelastic as the quantity demanded for investments in Singapore will change less than proportionately to a change in the interest rates. This also implies that factors affecting the MEI are more important determinants of the level of investments in Singapore.

> **Tip**
>
> Interest rate elasticity of demand for investments is similar to the concept of PED. Recall that PED measures the responsiveness of quantity demanded of a good to a change in price, ceteris paribus. Similarly, interest rate elasticity of investments measures the responsiveness of the quantity demanded for investments to a change in interest rates, ceteris paribus.

10. Explain the need for Real Gross National Product per capita.

Gross Domestic Product (GDP) refers to the market value of all final goods and services newly produced within a country in a given period of time (usually one year). Gross National Product (GNP) can be defined as the **market value of all final goods and services newly produced** anywhere in the world from resources belonging to residents of country in a given period of time (usually one year). In short, GDP refers to output produced within the geographical boundaries of a country, whereas GNP refers to output produced by factors of production owned by the nationals of a country.

GNP can be a more accurate measure of the material standard of living (SOL) for the average resident, especially in cases of developing economies. The economic growth in developing economies tend to be heavily driven by foreign direct investment (FDI). At the same time, their firms are unlikely to have expanded overseas via direct investment abroad (DIA) to earn incomes from overseas investments. This means that the net factor income from abroad is likely to be negative due to the profit repatriation outflow of money by FDI outweighing the profit repatriation inflow of money by DIA. Hence, the GDP of these economies may overstate their material SOL, because a large amount of incomes earned may be transferred overseas to the owner of these foreign firms as repatriated profits. Therefore the residents of the economy are not enjoying as much incomes and consumption as what the GDP figures may suggest. Due to GNP being the sum of GDP and net factor income from abroad i.e. GNP = GDP + net factor income from abroad, GNP is therefore a more accurate measure as it takes into account the negative net factor income from abroad.

However, GNP alone is an insufficient indicator of the material SOL as it **does not factor in the size of the population for comparison between economies.** For example, the GNP for China may be larger than most economies including Singapore's, but when divided by total population, it is a much smaller figure, indicating that the average person in China earns a lot lesser than the average person in Singapore. It also does not factor in **demographic changes** for comparison within an economy across different time periods, because if population increases more than the increase in GNP, the income of the average resident would have decreased even though national income has increased. Hence, **GNP per capita, which is** $\frac{\text{GNP}}{\text{Total Population}}$**, is necessary to factor in these**

demographic changes to determine if the material SOL for the average resident has indeed improved or deteriorated.

However, **GNP per capita does not take into account of changes in price levels**. Even though GNP may be increasing, the amount of output produced and purchasing power may not be increasing if the increase in GNP is due to higher prices. Hence, real GNP per capita is necessary to take into account of demographic changes and to **remove the effects of price changes, so that a more accurate measure of SOL can be obtained.**

Evaluation

While real GNP per capita takes into account demographic changes and inflation rates, it **does not account for non-material aspects of SOL**, such as pollution levels (air and water quality), amount of leisure and family time, as well as education standards and health conditions. People in a country with high real GNP per capita may have very poor non-material standard of living. Examples include Hong Kong and "cancer cities" in China whose residents suffer from toxic air despite enjoying strong economic growth. Economic growth has meant an increase in heavy industrial output which creates air and water pollution. These pollutants lower air and water quality as well as health standards and hence lowering non-material SOL.

A higher real GNP per capita may also be due to workers working longer hours and hence having less leisure time. This **hectic and fast-paced work-centric lifestyle can lead to enormous amounts of stress** that greatly diminish non-material SOL. Family units may experience internal friction and conflict due to these increased stress levels and lack of quality family time.

High real GNP per capita also does not take into account the resulting traffic congestion that may occur from economic growth. As incomes increase, the demand for car usage also increases, thereby resulting in traffic congestion. Traffic jams generally make people flustered and create inconveniences, thereby reducing their non-material SOL.

Moreover, Real GNP per capita fails to account for income inequality. Real GNP per capita only measures the average income earned by residents of a country. However, the income can be very unevenly distributed, and majority of the incomes could be concentrated in the hands of the already high incomers, a very small percentage of the population. It is therefore an insufficient measure of SOL, as even with increase in Real GNP per capita, the increase in incomes could be merely enjoyed by the few high income earners, while the majority are not experiencing an increase in real incomes and material SOL.

11. Explain the use of PPP exchange rate for cross country comparisons of real GDP per capita.

In order for a comparison of real GDP per capita to be made between countries, a **conversion to a common currency is necessary**. However, using exchange rates obtained from the currency market to convert the currencies **does not take into account the differences in the costs of living between countries.** In addition, these exchange rates are **determined by a variety of factors** that affect the demand and supply of a country's currency, such as speculative hot money flows and central bank intervention. Therefore, using these exchange rates would **not provide an accurate comparison of real GDP per capita**.

Although real GDP per capita already accounts for inflation and demographic changes, it cannot account for differing prices of goods and services between countries. For example, assume that both countries have the same exact value of Real GDP per capita, based on a common currency. However, one country's price levels are twice higher than another's. Hence their material standard of living is not the same, and in fact the residents of the country whose price levels are higher, can only enjoy half as many goods and services as the residents of the other country.

Therefore, to accurately compare material SOL across countries, the PPP exchange rate is used in order to **properly account for differences in costs of living between countries.**

PPP refers to the number of currency units of one country's currency required to purchase an amount of goods and services equivalent to what can be bought with one unit of the base currency in the base country. In most cases, US dollar is used as the base currency and US as the base country. Hence, PPP exchange rate is the rate of currency conversion that will allow one to buy the same basket of goods in each country using their domestic currency.

For example, PPP exchange rate between US and Singapore could be calculated by average price of a basket of goods and services in Singapore divided by average price of the same basket of goods and services in US.

$$PPP\ exchange\ rate = \frac{Average\ price\ of\ basket\ of\ goods\ and\ services\ in\ Singapore}{Average\ price\ of\ basket\ of\ goods\ and\ services\ in\ US}$$

According to the International Monetary Fund (IMF), the implied PPP exchange rate in Singapore for 2015 is 1.09 SGD per USD. This is in contrast to the exchange rates in the foreign exchange market which in 2015 is around 1.35 SGD per USD. What this implies is that using the exchange rate from the foreign exchange market would actually understate the material SOL in Singapore relative to the US.

Tip Candidates may be required to critically evaluate if the standard of living in a country has improved or deteriorated based on a given set of data. Knowledge on the necessity of real GNP or GDP per capita and adjustments using PPP can allow the candidate to recognize the limitations of certain forms of national income accounting and more accurately compare SOL across countries. For example, although real GNP is higher in China than in Singapore, we cannot necessarily conclude that SOL is higher in China than in Singapore as Singapore actually consists of a much lower population as compared to China. The average resident in Singapore actually earns more than the average resident in China and as such Singaporeans generally experience greater material SOL than the Chinese. However, when adjusted for PPP, the gap in material SOL narrows as the costs of living in China is much lower than the costs of living in Singapore. Hence, knowledge of real GNP per capita after adjusting for PPP is essential in helping us compare standard of living across countries.

12. Explain the multiplier effect.

The multiplier effect occurs when an **increase in autonomous spending** results in a greater **increase in real national income (RNY) with respect to the initial increase in spending.** The general idea behind the multiplier effect is that any initial increase in autonomous spending will increase RNY and induce an increase in consumption, which further increases RNY, resulting in multiple rounds of spending and income generation. Essentially, this is due to the fact that one person's spending is another person's income. Hence, the final increase in RNY is a multiplied amount of the initial increase in spending.

The **multiplier effect** can be triggered by any **increase in injections (J)**; namely any autonomous increases in investments (I), government spending (G) or export revenue (X). It can also be triggered by a **fall in withdrawals (W)**; namely any fall in taxes (T), import expenditure (M) and savings (S), which will correspond with an increase in domestic consumption (Cd).

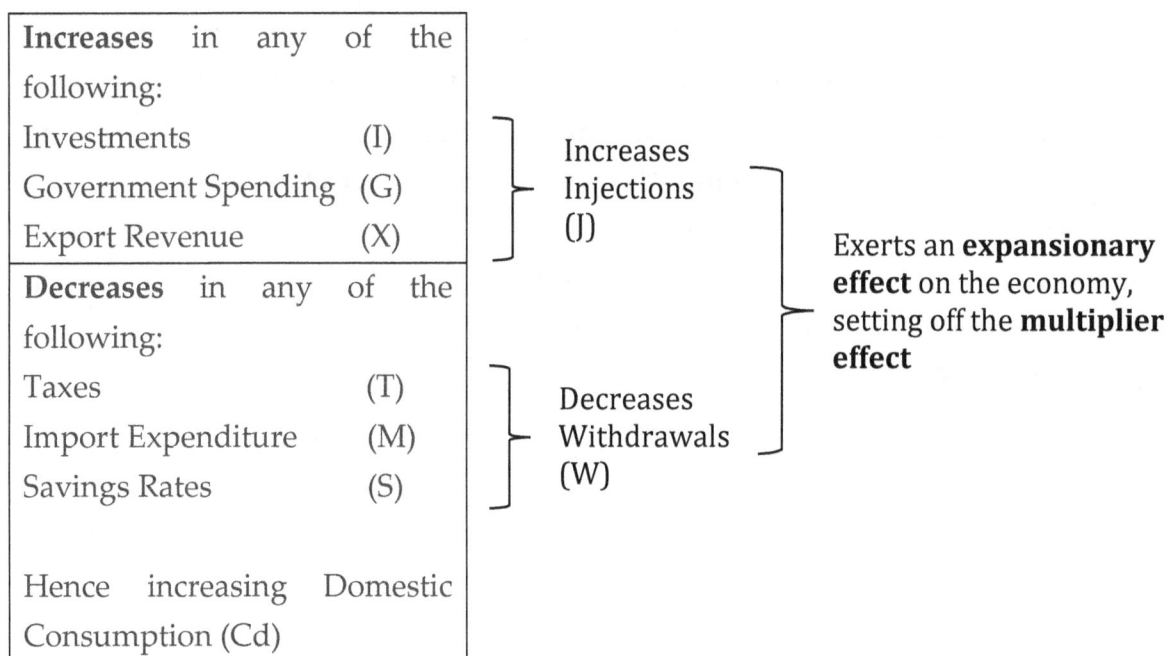

Increases in any of the following:		
Investments	(I)	
Government Spending	(G)	Increases Injections (J)
Export Revenue	(X)	
Decreases in any of the following:		
Taxes	(T)	
Import Expenditure	(M)	Decreases Withdrawals (W)
Savings Rates	(S)	
Hence increasing Domestic Consumption (Cd)		

Exerts an **expansionary effect** on the economy, setting off the **multiplier effect**

Conversely, the **reverse multiplier effect** can be triggered by a **decrease in J**; namely a fall in I, G or X. It can also be triggered by an **increase in W**; namely an increase in T, M or S, which will correspond with a fall in Cd.

Decreases in any of the following: Investments (I) Government Spending (G) Export Revenue (X)	Decreases Injections (J)
Increases in any of the following: Taxes (T) Import Expenditure (M) Savings Rates (S) Hence decreasing Domestic Consumption (Cd)	Increases Withdrawals (W)

Exerts an **contractionary effect** on the economy, setting off the **reverse multiplier effect**

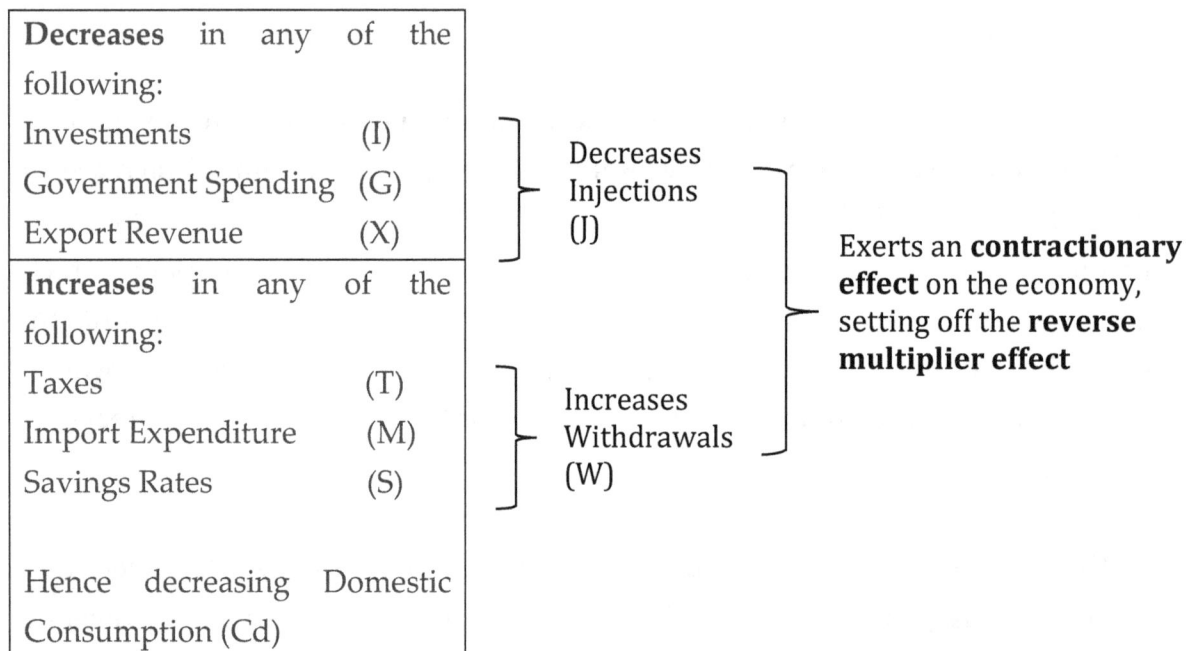

Extent of increase in RNY – Size of K

The extent to which RNY increases as a result of the multiplier effect depends on the **marginal propensity to consume domestic goods and services (MPCd)**. The MPCd measures the **proportion of additional income** that households will **use for consumption of domestically produced goods and services.** For example, if a household earns an additional \$1, saves \$0.10, spends \$0.10 on imported goods, pays \$0.10 in taxes, and spends the remaining \$0.70 on domestically produced goods and services, the household's MPCd is 0.7. This means that for every additional dollar earned, the household will spend \$0.70 on domestically produced goods and services. This is why the multiplier effect has a limit and will eventually peter out, or end, **because every subsequent round of spending results in a smaller amount (0.7) being re-injected into the economy, while 0.3 of every increase in RNY is leaked out of the circular flow of income.** The process will stop when the amount of W will increase to match the increased level of J, and a new national income equilibrium is achieved.

$$MPCd = \frac{\Delta Cd}{\Delta RNY} = \frac{\textbf{Change in domestic consumption}}{\textbf{Change in RNY}}$$

The size of the multiplier takes the value of **k**, where

$$k = \frac{1}{1 - MPCd} = \frac{1}{MPW} = \frac{1}{MPM + MPT + MPS} = \frac{Change\ in\ GDP}{Change\ in\ Autonomous\ Spending}$$

The **higher the value of the multiplier, the more RNY is increased by an initial increase in autonomous spending.** If the size of k = 5, an initial increase in government spending of 1 billion will lead to an increase in national income of 5 billion.

The formula for the total increase in national income can be computed by **Change in Real National Income** = k x (increase in autonomous spending), where k is the multiplier value.

AD-AS analysis

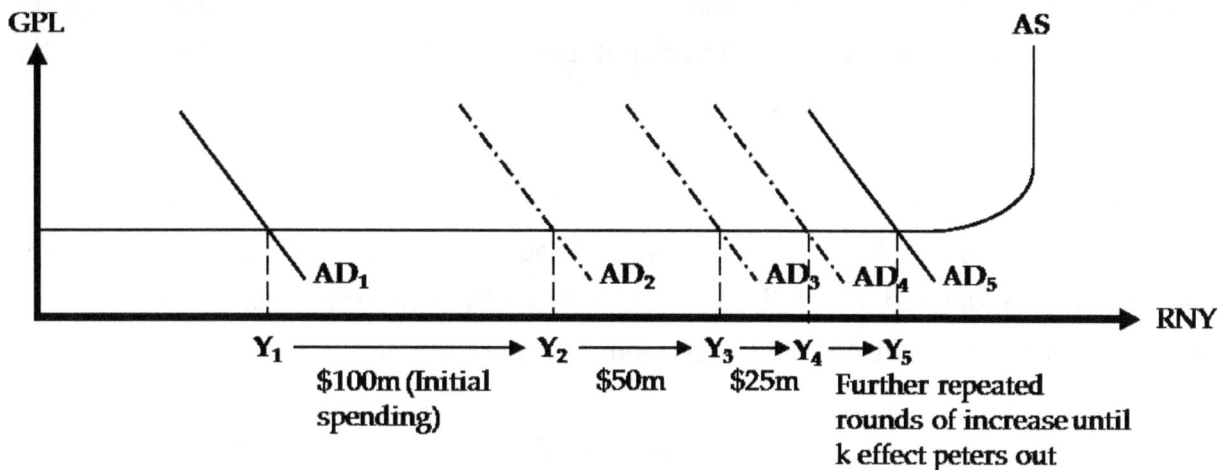

Fig 1: Multiplier Effect

For the following explanation of the multiplier effect, refer to Fig 1. Assuming that there was an autonomous increase in spending of $100m due to an increase in government expenditure on public works projects, this increases AD from AD_1 to AD_2 and national income by $100m from Y_1 to Y_2 as the government pays for construction services to complete these jobs. Factor owners involved in rendering these construction services, such as construction workers, owners of construction firms etc, will experience an increase in their incomes by $100m and spend 50% of it, assuming MPCd = 0.5, inducing an increase in consumption by $50m. This results in a further increase in AD from AD_2 to AD_2 while the remaining $50m gets leaked out of the economy in the form of T, M and S. The increase in consumption will lead to unplanned decreases in stocks and inventories of firms, leading firms to increase production, and hiring more workers in the process. Therefore, the increase in consumption by $50m has led to a further increase of RNY by $50mil from Y_2 to Y_3 as factor owners earn an increase in income due to the increase in consumption. This $50m increase in national income further induces an increase in consumption by $25m, increasing AD from AD_3 to AD_4 while households experience a further increase in national income of $25m from Y_3 to Y_4. This cycle of spending and income-generation continues until AD_5 is reached and RNY is at Y_5, as the process stops when there is no more additional spending. This occurs when the increase in withdrawals equal the increase in injections as the initial increase in government spending has fully leaked out of the circular flow of income.

Since the formula relating the change in national income and the multiplier goes by (change in national income) = k x (change in AE), since the multiplier value is 2 (given that MPC is 0.5), the final change in national income will be 2x100m = $200m from the initial $100m in government spending.

Evaluation

The extent of the multiplier effect in bringing about a multiplied increase in RNY when AD increases is dependent on the current state of the economy, availability of spare capacity and the range of AS that the economy is operating at.

Due to abundance of spare capacity n the Keynesian range, a rise in AD need not lead to a rise in GPL. As GPL stays constant at P, the multiple rounds of induced consumption, arising from the initial autonomous increase in AD, can occur to the fullest extent. This is because the increase in households' real incomes is not mitigated by erosion in purchasing power by inflation and falling real value of money. Hence the economy experiences the full multiplier effect.

The intermediate range results in a smaller multiplier effect. Because of a supply bottleneck and competition for resources resulting in firms bidding up prices for them, GPL begins to increase. The increase in prices deters consumption and hence, induced consumption does not increase by as much compared to at the Keynesian range, and there is only a partial multiplier effect where real GDP increases by a lesser extent than expected.

In the classical range, however, there is zero multiplier effect as any increase in AD does not result in an increase in real GDP or real national incomes, since resources are already fully employed. Hence any increase in AD is unable to trigger subsequent rounds of induced consumption and the multiplier process. There will only be an increase in the GPL, as firms compete for resources to increase production as a result of excess demand. However, no increase in Real GDP occurs as resources are merely shifted away from one industry to another.

13. Explain the usefulness of knowing the size of the multiplier.

Marginal propensity to consume (**MPCd**), refers to **proportion of additional income that a consumer will use for consumption of domestically produced goods and services**. Marginal propensity to withdraw (**MPW**) refers to the **proportion of every unit increase in national income that is spent on imported goods and services, taxed, or saved.** Marginal propensity to import (MPM) refers to the proportion of every unit increase in national income that is spent on imports. Marginal propensity to tax (MPT) refers to the proportion of every unit increase in national income that is taxed. Marginal propensity to save (MPS) refers to the proportion of every unit increase in national income that is saved.

The size of the multiplier takes the value of **k**, where

$$k = \frac{1}{1 - MPCd} = \frac{1}{MPW} = \frac{1}{MPM + MPT + MPS} = \frac{Change\ in\ GDP}{Change\ in\ Autonomous\ Spending}$$

Therefore the smaller the MPCd, the larger the MPW and the smaller the size of the multiplier. The converse is true. The **higher the value of the multiplier, the more real national income (RNY) is increased by an initial increase in autonomous spending.**

Total Change in RNY = k x (Initial Change in Aggregate Expenditure)

If the k value is 2, an initial increase in spending of 1 million leads to an increase in RNY of 2 million. If the k value is 4, an initial increase in spending of 1 million leads to an increase in RNY of 4 million.

Knowing the size of the multiplier can allow us to evaluate the effectiveness of macroeconomic policies. Furthermore, it helps the government determine how much they should change spending or taxes in order to achieve the desired macroeconomic objectives.

In countries with a **large multiplier, expansionary fiscal and monetary policies** tend to be **more effective** as the multiplier effect works to effect **a greater increase in RNY relative to the initial increase in spending.** (Similarly, these countries can use contractionary demand management policies more effectively to reduce inflationary pressures, since the **reverse-multiplier effect** will result in a **greater decrease in AD and hence GPL relative to the initial fall in spending**.)

In contrast, demand management policies in countries with a **small multiplier** will be less effective. Countries that have a large MPW, usually due to higher tax rates, a culture of thrift, and greater import reliance will have a smaller multiplier value. These countries will hence **have to consider supporting the expansionary demand management policies with short-term supply-side policies as well, in order to achieve the desired change in national income or general price levels.** Alternatively, these countries **can pursue more aggressive demand-management policies**. For example, government spending must be increased a lot more aggressively to effect the desired increase in national income.

However, having a **high multiplier value is a double-edged sword**. While a high multiplier leads to greater effectiveness of demand-management policies, it also means that the **effects of a recession will be more prominent in such countries**. Any autonomous fall in spending will set forth a greater reverse-multiplier effect and hence lead to a **larger decrease in RNY** as compared to countries with a smaller multiplier value. Likewise, all else being equal, these countries may also be more vulnerable to demand-pull inflation when there is an autonomous increase in spending.

Tip

It is imperative to note that fiscal and monetary policies are not useless in countries with a small multiplier. These policies still work, but they are just less effective as compared to an economy with a higher multiplier value.

14. Explain how economic growth may harm the standard of living.

Standard of living (SOL) refers to the economic and social well-being of the people in a certain country. It can be classified into material and non-material aspects. Material SOL refers to the quantity and quality of material goods and services enjoyed while non-material SOL is concerned about the intangible quality of life factors including the amount of leisure time, health and education standards, air quality etc. Economic growth may harm both material and non-material SOL.

As the economy experiences **economic growth, inflation** may occur. If **inflation rates exceed the rate of wage increase**, workers will experience a **fall in real wages**. Due to this fall in real wage, they will be less able to **consume goods and services**. As such, material SOL falls. This especially affects fixed income earners such as pensioners and often unskilled workers.

Economic growth can also lead to greater **income inequality**. Since economic growth may occur as a result of **economic restructuring** whereby **certain industries with comparative advantage expand while others decline**. As such, this will result in a **higher demand for workers who possess skills in those booming industries**, while demand for workers in declining industries decrease, leading to lower wages and even structural unemployment. Hence, certain segments of the population may actually experience a fall in SOL.

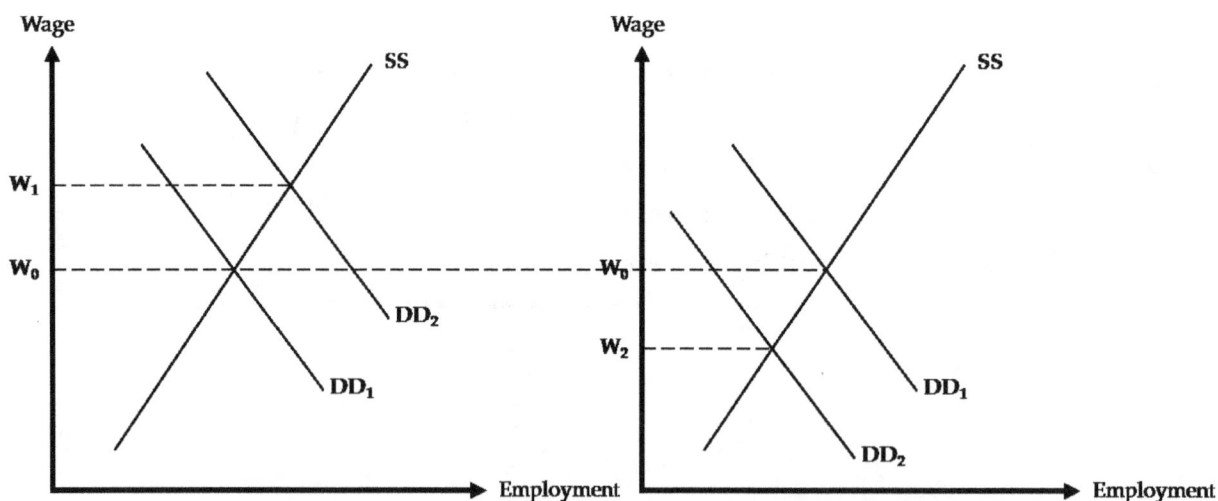

Fig 1: Expanding Industry Labour Market   Fig 2: Declining Industry Labour Market

Referring to Fig 1 and 2, assume that both industries offer similar wages at W_0 initially. However, in the pursuit of economic growth, the economy may now be opened up to trade, and there is an **increase in demand for workers who possess the skills to work in the expanding industry in which there is comparative advantage,** from DD_1 to DD_2 in Fig 1. As demand increases, this exerts an upwards pressure on wages to increase from W_0 to W_1. In declining industries, demand for workers falls from DD_1 to DD_2 in Fig 2, and this will exert a downward pressure on wages, causing wages to decrease from W_0 to W_2. Hence, workers in expanding industries earn higher wages while workers in declining industries receive lower wages. At the same time, structural unemployment may also occur as workers that are laid off in the declining industry do not possess the skills to work in the expanding industry. As such, **income inequality and structural unemployment occurs while economic growth is achieved.** The resulting fall in wages and rising structural unemployment in these declining industries means that these **workers are no longer able to consume as much as before. Hence, their material SOL falls.** Their reduced consumption may also mean that they consume fewer goods and services such as those related to education and healthcare, hence possibly resulting in a fall in non-material SOL.

As an economy **experiences growth, her workers may be working longer hours and facing higher workload. These will result in less leisure and family time. Hence, non-material SOL falls.**

Furthermore, since economic growth means there is **increased production**, this could lead to **more pollutants being released into the environment** by production plants and factories, resulting in greater pollution of the air, rivers, lakes and the sea. Air pollution causes **respiratory problems** like asthma, while smog results in breathing difficulties. Water pollution by **hazardous chemicals** are passed on to humans when fish or other wildlife consume these chemicals, thereby causing health problems and decreasing non-material SOL.

Economic growth can also lead to **congestion and increased strain on social fabric**. If the reason for economic growth is due to an influx of foreign workers for their low-cost labour, the resultant increase in population can result in **greater congestion** on the roads, on public transport, in shopping centres, hospitals and in community spaces. Furthermore, the **influx of foreign workers could be straining on the social fabric of society** as the locals and foreign workers may not get along. This could be due to differences in cultural backgrounds, habits, and the perception that foreign workers are competing against the locals for jobs. Hence, despite greater purchasing power and material SOL, stress levels may rise and **non-material SOL deteriorates.**

Evaluation

It is true that economic growth can indeed bring with it **many negative externalities** that may compromise a country's SOL. However, despite these downsides, society should still continue to pursue economic growth since a lack of growth would most likely lead to rising unemployment, which may require more government spending on welfare benefits while tax revenues remain stagnant due to stagnant national incomes. This could reduce the government's ability to implement policies to improve non-material SOL. For example, the provision of merit and public goods such as education and parks may be compromised. Without economic growth, material SOL would also be stagnant or falling as population continues to grow. Hence, **without economic growth, both material and non-material SOL will be severely compromised**. It must therefore be conceded that economic growth is desirable and generally leads to increased SOL. In order to mitigate the costs that come with economic growth, it should be accompanied with **specific policies undertaken to reduce the problem of negative externalities, and increase its inclusiveness to ensure more sustainable and equitable growth.**

15. Explain how structural unemployment comes about.

Structural unemployment refers to unemployment which arises because segments of the labour force do not possess the skill sets that industries in a country demand or require. It is a situation of a **persistent mismatch between the skills possessed by workers and the skills demanded by industries.**

Firstly, **changes in comparative advantage** can cause massive structural unemployment. For example, the **US has lost comparative advantage in labour intensive manufacturing due to the emergence of low-cost economies like China and India.** These economies possess greater factor endowment of cheap labour and hence have comparative advantage in producing low-end, low-skilled labour intensive goods. As such, these industries in the US have declined and firms have relocated to economies like China and India. Many workers who are unemployed may lack skills to work in the new sectors such as ecommerce, which the US has comparative advantage in.

The **advent of new technology** can result in discovery of certain production techniques like using robotics, which reduces cost and increases efficiency, rendering human labour obsolete. For example, industrial robots are displacing workers in the manufacturing industry. Workers that are laid off may lack skills to work in other growth sectors. Similarly, computers and electronic data bases have also reduced the number of clerks required for book-keeping and other administrative functions.

Geographical immobility can also result in structural unemployment. Due to the decline of industries in certain regions of the country, unemployment occurs. However, job vacancies are actually available in other regions of the country yet those unemployed may not be able to or willing to leave their hometown and move to regions where there are jobs, possibly due to an inadequate transportation infrastructure, high moving costs, high costs of living or rootedness in their hometown due to family relationships. Hence, although there are job vacancies in other areas, these workers remain unemployed.

Comparative Advantage is ever-changing and it is possible for governments to "create" new areas of comparative advantage by actively altering factors of production. In Singapore, this has been achieved through educational policies such as the compulsory education system and supply-side policies like re-training programs. These have helped equip workers with new and relevant skills in the production of high-end, high value-added products.

Evaluation

Ultimately, structural unemployment tends to be **long-term and the most difficult type of unemployment to solve, imposing significant economic and social costs**. Workers who have been structurally unemployed may have fixed mindsets which may make it difficult for them to be retrained or to relocate to a new geographical area. As such, many jobs remain out of reach for them. Much also depends on their aptitude for the new skills in demand, and the lower the level of education, the more difficult it is to retain a worker.

However, the extent of structural unemployment can still be lowered by **constant skills updating and retraining programmes**. These supply-side policies will be able to better equip phased-out workers with new and more relevant skills to reduce structural unemployment.

Nevertheless, some amount of structural unemployment is unavoidable in any dynamic and growing economy. This is because in any vibrant economy, industries expand and decline, while technology is constantly progressing.

16. Explain how demand-pull inflation occurs.

Inflation is defined as a **sustained increase** in the **general price level (GPL)** of goods and services in an economy. Demand-pull inflation occurs when aggregate demand (AD) is increasing in excess of aggregate supply (AS). Typically, there is a **sustained increase** in AD when the **economy is operating at or near full capacity.**

Keynesian View

The Keynesian view holds that for demand-pull inflation to occur, AD rises due to an increase in either C, I, G or (X-M), resulting in higher GPL. Factors that lead to an increase in expenditure on domestically produced goods and services can therefore result in demand-pull inflation.

Monetarist View

The Monetarist view holds that demand-pull inflation occurs when there is an excessive increase in money supply, resulting in an increase in AD as people have more money to consume goods and services. This results in a situation where there is too much money chasing too few goods, thereby leading to higher prices.

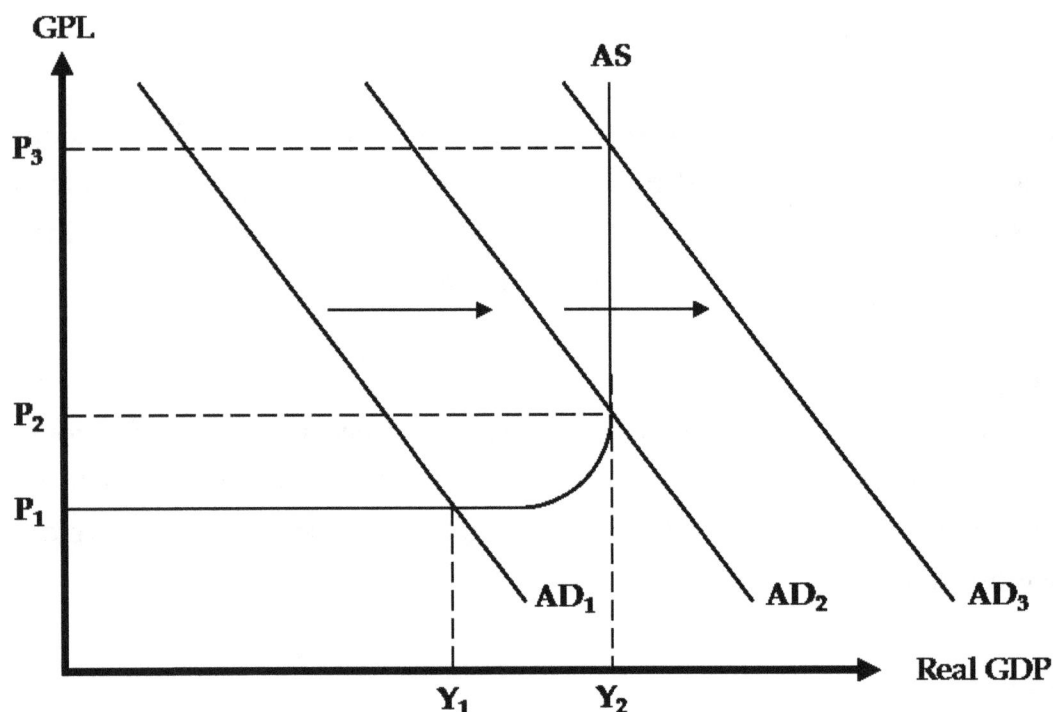

Fig 1: Demand-pull Inflation

Due to the increase in AD as shown in Fig 1 from AD_1 to AD_2 to AD_3, excess demand for goods and services occur, leading to the bidding up of prices by households, firms, government and foreigners. Firms experience an **unexpected decrease in stocks and inventories**, and will hence **demand more factor inputs to increase production** in order to meet the increased demand for goods and services. However, since the economy is **already operating near full capacity**, there is a **supply bottleneck** as fewer and **fewer scarce resources** are now available. Most workers are employed while other factor inputs are already being used. Firms therefore have to **compete over these factors of production**, offering higher wages to workers and higher prices for raw materials. This will **drive up factor prices** and increase unit costs of production, thereby leading **to higher prices of goods and services** and hence, inflation. All these will lead to an increase in GPL from P_1 to P_2 to P_3.

Evaluation

Beneficial Effects

However, demand-pull inflation is caused by increasing AD which can be **beneficial to an economy** as it can boost economic growth and employment. Referring to Fig 1, as AD increases from AD_1 to AD_2 and GPL increases from P_1 to P_2, employment also increases as real GDP increases from Y_1 to Y_2. This results in **economic growth** and **greater levels of national income**. However, if the economy is already **operating at full capacity Y_2**, any further increase in AD, such as that from AD_2 to AD_3, **will not result in an increase in employment or national income**. This is due to the fact that all available factors of production are already employed and hence, there **is no spare capacity to increase output.** In such an instance, an increase in AD will only bring about **inflation with no economic growth**. Hence, inflation in this case is **undesirable.**

If demand-pull inflation occurs at low rates (around 3-4%), this can be seen as a sign of a healthy, booming economy. With strong business confidence, investments may increase. Moreover, as prices increase due to rising AD, firms also usually experience an increase in profit margins. This occurs because the rise in factor prices like wages usually lags behind the increase in prices paid by consumers. This could be due to existing fixed wage contracts. With increased profits, firms have more funds for investments, and with higher profit margins, expected rate of return on investment projects also increase hence increasing investments. The rise in investments will not only increase AD and contribute to more actual growth, but will also add even more capital stock to the economy, thereby increasing potential growth.

Different Root Causes

The **root cause of inflation also differs between countries**. Countries like Singapore that are **heavily export-oriented** with low domestic consumption are likely to experience demand-pull **inflation due to an increase in net exports**. However, in recent years, the increase in money supply due to the massive quantitative easing by countries like the US has also led to demand-pull inflation in Singapore. On the other hand, demand-pull inflation in countries like China and India is also significantly contributed by **massive inflows of foreign direct investments** due to their **factor endowments** in cheap labour and land. Hence, knowing the context and make-up of the economy will allow us to effectively **discern the most pertinent cause of demand-pull inflation** and how to best tackle it.

Demand Pull versus Cost Push

In general, **demand-pull inflation is usually preferred to cost-push inflation** as demand-pull inflation is caused by rising AD and hence, reflects a growing economy. In contrast, cost-push inflation is caused by a rise in unit costs of production and can instead lead to negative economic growth on top of higher GPL. However, demand-pull inflation can also lead to much greater levels of income inequality. The poor tend to earn fixed incomes and will hence have the real value of their incomes eroded by inflation. In contrast, the rich tend to earn variable incomes which may now be increasing if their incomes are pegged to the revenues and profits of firms. Hence their real incomes may be increasing or at least more protected against inflation. This therefore results in worsening income inequality.

17. Explain how cost-push inflation occurs.

Cost-push inflation can be defined as inflation caused by falling aggregate supply (AS). Cost push inflation may occur when an **increase in prices of factor inputs, land, labour, capital and entrepreneurship reduces short-run aggregate supply (SRAS)** and results in **higher general price levels (GPL)**.

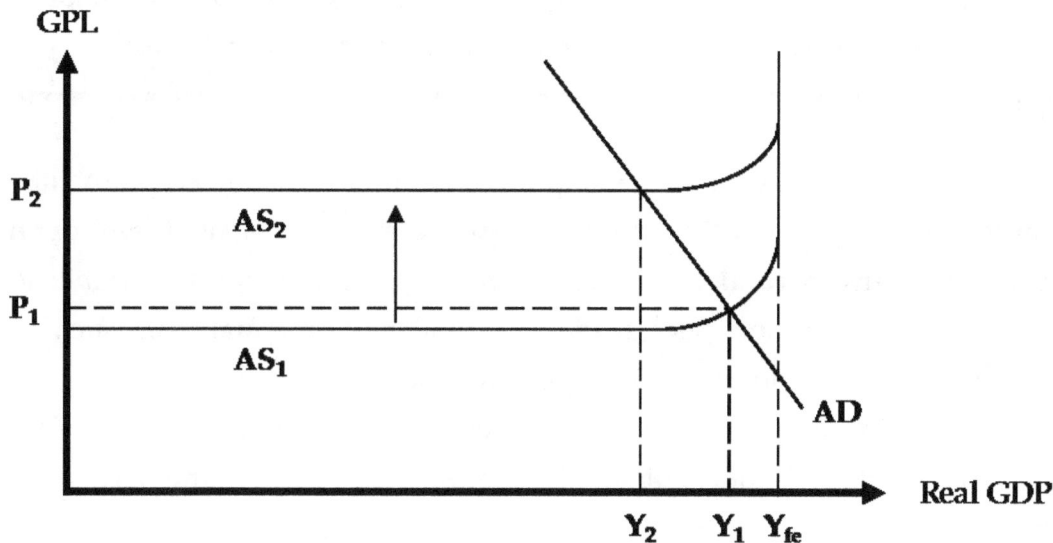

Fig 1: Cost-push Inflation from Falling SRAS

For example, it may be due to widespread increase in wages. Wages usually constitute a significant proportion of production costs. Hence, as **wages of workers increase without a corresponding increase in productivity, unit costs of production increase** as firms have to pay more to workers for the same amount of output. This results in a **fall in the SRAS** as represented by an upwards shift in AS curve from AS_1 to AS_2 since firms are willing and able to produce less at every given price level. Firms will pass on the increased costs of production to consumers by **charging higher prices**, resulting in an increase in GPL from P_1 to P_2 and thus causing cost-push inflation. This form of cost-push inflation can also be referred to as wage-push inflation.

However, if productivity increases more than wages, there will not be any wage-push inflation. This is because workers will be able to produce more relative to what they are paid, which leads to a fall in unit labour costs. This fall in unit labour costs and hence unit cost of production leads to an increase in SRAS from AS_2 to AS_1. Therefore, GPL falls from P_2 to P_1. Wage increases will not always lead to inflation, especially if productivity increases more than or at the same rate as wage increases.

At times, the cost-push inflation may be imported, especially in an economy like Singapore that is heavily dependent on imported raw materials. As a **small and open economy** with **hardly any natural resources**, Singapore is extremely susceptible to world prices as she has to **import necessities like food and raw materials such as crude oil**. If world food prices increase, Singapore will be adversely hit as she has no choice but to continue importing these items as they are necessary for her survival. Similarly, Singapore needs to **import substantial amounts of primary and secondary inputs for her production**. About 60% of the value of her exports is made up of imported content. Therefore, if the price of oil, an essential input for many manufacturing industries as well as for energy and transport services, increases, the cost of production will also increase across the economy and hence lead to cost-push inflation. This form of cost-push inflation is also considered to be imported inflation.

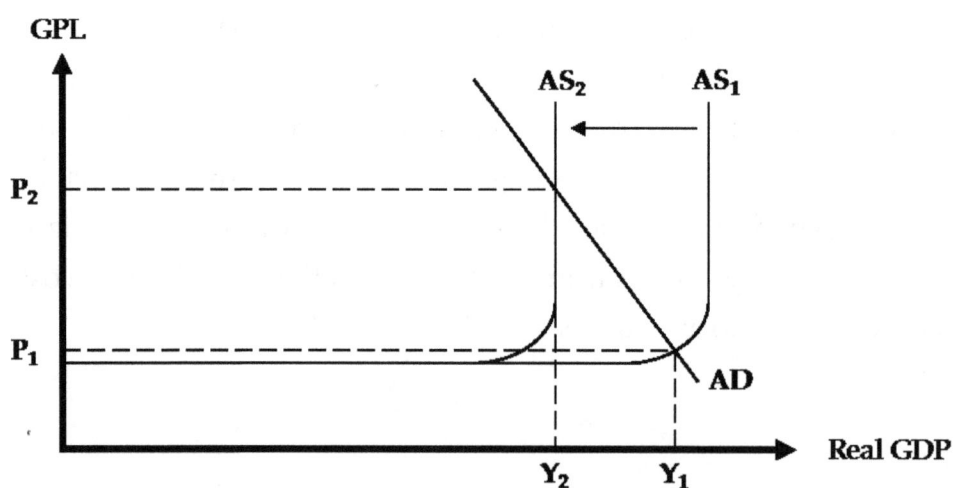

Fig 2: Cost-push Inflation from Falling LRAS

A **fall in productive capacity** can also lead to cost-push inflation. If a natural disaster like an earthquake or tsunami leads to the destruction of many fixed assets and infrastructure, the economy will experience a **decrease in its quantity of resources**. There are now fewer factors of production available. The fall in LRAS is represented by a leftward shift in AS from AS_1 to AS_2 in Fig 2. This may lead to **greater competition by firms** for the now scarcer resources, resulting in **higher unit costs of production**. These increased costs of production are passed on to consumers which results in an increase in general price level from P_1 to P_2, thereby leading to **cost-push inflation**.

As the government **levies indirect taxes on goods and services** (e.g. sales taxes in the US), firms will face an **increase in unit costs of production**, part of which will be passed on to consumers, resulting in cost-push inflation.

An increase in market power especially of firms belonging to certain critical industries like utilities and telecommunications can also lead to cost-push inflation. These industries tend to be natural monopolies due to the very high start-up costs and presence of very large economies of scale. If unregulated, these firms with **greater monopoly power** will be able to quite easily charge higher prices in order to earn more monopoly profits. They can also quite easily **pass on any increased costs** to consumers in order to **preserve or even increase their profits**. Since utilities and communications are used by the entire economy, this leads to an increase in the unit cost of production for all industries and hence cost-push inflation. This form of cost-push inflation can also be referred to as profit-push inflation.

18. Explain the wage-price spiral.

Wage-price spiral is a **vicious cycle** where both **firms and unions attempt to protect their real incomes** against inflation which results in **continuous increases in general price levels (GPL)**.

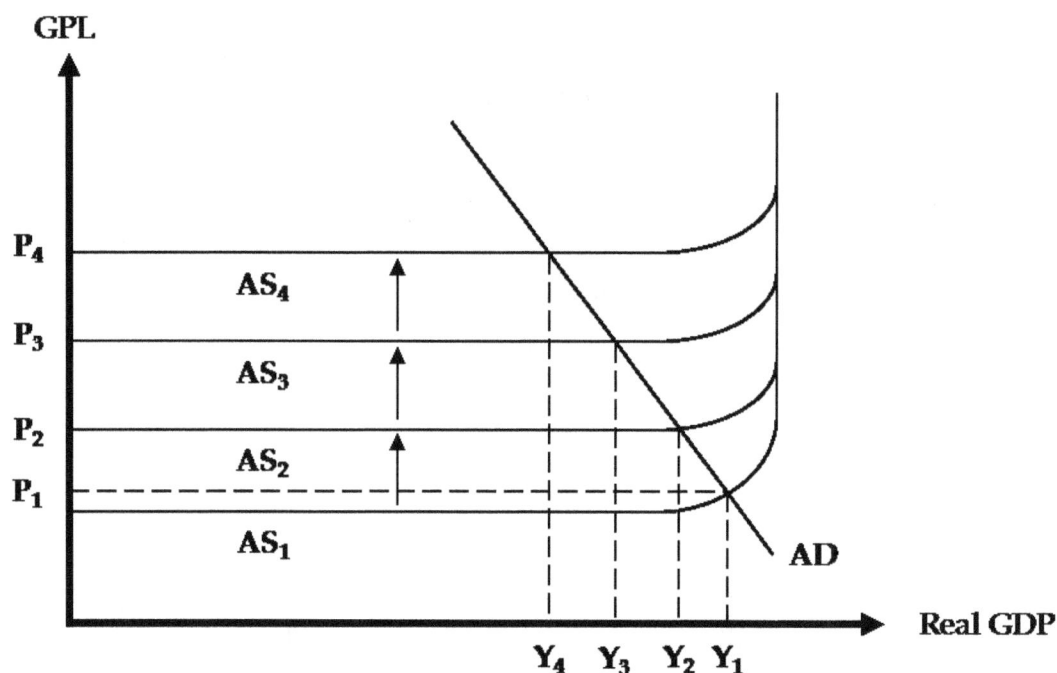

Fig 1: Wage-price spiral

Wage-price spiral begins with an **initial increase in GPL**. This can be caused by either demand-pull inflation or cost-push inflation, such as a possible supply shock when shortage of oil leads to rising oil prices. This fall in SRAS is represented by an upward shift in AS curve from AS_1 to AS_2 in Fig 1, resulting in inflation and rising GPL from P_1 to P_2.

As GPL increases, **purchasing power of workers fall**. This is because workers continue earning the same incomes while goods and services have become more expensive. These workers are **hence unable to afford as much goods and services with the same level of income**. Workers and trade unions will **start bargaining for higher wages**, so as to regain their previous level of real incomes, and if they succeed, there will be an **increase in unit labour costs and hence unit costs of production**. Due to higher costs of production, firms will **attempt to pass on the higher costs of production to consumers**. This causes SRAS to fall, which is represented by an upward shift in AS from AS_2 to AS_3 in Fig 1, with a further rise in GPL from P_2 to P_3.

As GPL increases, workers will **once again face lower real incomes** and **begin another round of bargaining** for higher wages in order to protect their real incomes. This causes SRAS to fall once again, and is represented by an upward shift in AS from AS_3 to AS_4, resulting in yet another increase in GPL from P_3 to P_4. Therefore a **vicious cycle of prices chasing up wages and wages chasing up prices** – a **wage-price spiral ensues.**

Evaluation

If the economy is near or at full employment, firms are more likely to give in to the workers and unions' demands as it is difficult to hire other workers since almost everyone is already employed. Therefore there is a strong possibility that demand-pull inflation can easily lead to a wage-price spiral.

The likelihood of a wage-price spiral is also determined by the strength of labour unions in the country. For example, countries in the EU have a legal system protecting the rights of workers to protest and organize strikes to express their discontent. This has resulted in high wage increases that surpass their productivity growth, and is a key reason for the loss of their export price competitiveness, with the exception of Germany. In contrast, the Singapore government enacts laws that prohibit labour strikes and demonstrations. She also emphasizes a harmonious and collaborative tripartite relationship between the government, trade unions and employers, as seen in the National Wages Council which issues wage guidelines in consultation with employers, unions and government. As such, agitation for wage increases rarely occurs and wage-price spirals are averted.

19. Explain how inflation hurts economic growth and employment.

Inflation refers to a sustained increase in general price levels (GPL) in an economy. Economic growth can take the form of actual growth or potential growth. Actual growth refers to the increase in the amount of real output actually produced by the economy. Potential growth refers to the rate at which the productive capacity of the economy, or potential real output increases. The employment rate is the percentage of the labour force (total number of people of working age and who are willing and able to work) who is employed at a given point in time.

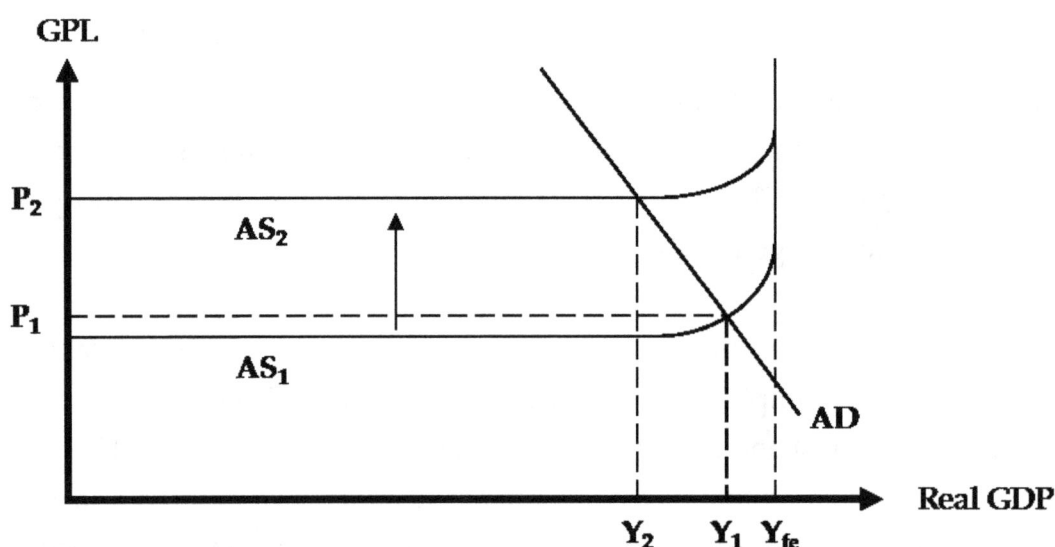

Fig 1: Cost-push Inflation

Cost-push inflation can result in a fall in real GDP and hence a fall in employment. An **increase in GPL** from P_1 to P_2 in Fig 1 has **resulted from a decrease in the short-run aggregate supply (SRAS)** which is represented by an upward shift from AS_1 to AS_2. This could be due to either an **increase in wages** or **prices of other factor inputs.** As the unit cost of production increases, firms **are not willing and able to produce as much as before** and will hence **cut back on production**, while also attempting to pass on some of the costs increases to consumers, leading to higher prices. As prices increase, the total quantity demanded of goods and services falls resulting in a fall in equilibrium real national output from Y_1 to Y_2 and since less output is being produced, firms lay off workers, increasing unemployment rate. This can therefore lead to a situation of stagflation – a stagnant economy facing both high inflation rates and high unemployment rates.

Furthermore, high and unstable inflation rates will **cause uncertainty** in an economy. Firms will be uncertain about prices of output as well as input, which will cause a **fall in their expected rate of return** due to the **increased risk of investing**. Hence, the **level of investments will decrease**. This can cause a fall in the aggregate demand (AD), leading to a fall in real GDP and employment levels. Furthermore, the fall in investments also reduces potential growth as it means that there is a fall in the rate of accumulation of capital goods. Therefore, long term economic growth prospects are also reduced.

Evaluation

However, mild demand-pull inflation can actually promote rather than reduce economic growth. With mild demand-pull inflation, firms can be growing in confidence about business prospects as this is an indicator of growing AD. The rising prices can also mean higher profit margins, as costs of production may not be increasing as quickly initially, for example due to fixed wage contracts. These lead to higher expected rates of return on investment projects, leading to higher levels of investments, hence promoting both actual and potential growth.

20. Explain how high rates of inflation can lead to deterioration of Balance of Trade and Balance of Payments.

Inflation refers to a sustained increase in general price levels (GPL) in an economy. A country's Balance of Payments (BOP) is an accounting statement that shows a country's economic transactions with the rest of the world. It is the net balance of all the inflows and outflows of money for the country. Inflows represent a receipt of payment from other countries while outflows represent a payment to other countries. The BOP comprises of the Current Account (CA) and the Capital and Financial Account (KFA). The Balance of Trade (BOT) is the largest component of the CA and refers to the difference between a country's export revenue (X), which are inflows, and import expenditure (M), which are outflows. The BOT is positive and in surplus if the country's export revenues (X) exceed its import expenditures (M).

The higher prices of domestically produced goods and services (due to inflation) will result in **imports becoming relatively cheaper** compared to domestically produced goods and services. As such, assuming that domestically produced goods and imports have positive cross elasticities and that they are **substitutes**, consumers will **increase demand for imports,** and hence **M rises.** Concurrently, **exports become relatively more expensive** compared to foreign produced goods and services, **losing export price competitiveness** and hence, assuming demand for exports is price-elastic, foreigners will reduce quantity demanded for this country's exports more than proportionately and **X falls.** Since M rises and X falls, **BOT deteriorates.**

Inflation resulting from higher prices of factor inputs will lead to increases in unit costs of production, **decreasing the expected rate of return on investments** in the country. This will **deter and decrease foreign direct investments (FDI).** Concurrently, local firms that **have lost confidence in the domestic economy will seek to invest abroad instead,** thereby **increasing direct investments abroad (DIA).** The fall in FDI and increase in DIA leads to a **deterioration of the KFA.**

Furthermore, inflation generally results in **greater levels of uncertainty over the prices of inputs and products.** This implies greater risk which lowers the expected rate of return on investment projects, **discouraging the inflow of FDI.**

As a result of a fall in inflows comprising X and FDI, the **demand for domestic currency will fall**. The increased outflows comprising M and DIA will lead to an increase in the supply of domestic currency so as to obtain more foreign currencies. The increase in supply and fall in demand will lead to a depreciation of the currency, resulting in exchange rate instability. A loss of confidence over the exchange rate, with increased expectations of further depreciations will result in increased **hot money outflows** and reduced hot money inflows as currency investors seek to invest in other currencies that will yield a higher expected rate of return. Hence, the KFA can be expected to deteriorate further.

With a deterioration in the BOT and hence the CA, as well as the KFA, high rates of inflation will therefore lead to a deterioration of the BOP.

Evaluation

However, if inflation rates are mild, this could be a sign of a booming economy. This could attract more FDI inflows and hence, KFA may improve, resulting in an improvement in the BOP. Furthermore, if inflation is demand-pull in nature, caused by an increase in (X-M), BOT is unlikely to deteriorate.

21. Explain how inflation may worsen income and wealth inequality.

Income inequality refers to the **difference in income between the rich and the poor**. The most common measure of income inequality is the GINI coefficient, where the higher the value, in a range from 0 to 1, represents greater income inequality. Wealth inequality refers to the difference in the amount of wealth between the rich and the poor.

Demand-pull inflation can contribute to income inequality. Demand-pull inflation may result in **greater profits for firms** since the aggregate demand and prices are rising. The rising prices can lead to higher profit margins, as costs of production increase at a slower rate compared to market prices. This could for example be due to fixed wage contracts. As inflation occurs, workers' fixed wages lose purchasing power and hence, real wages have fallen. **Firm owners therefore experience an increase in real profits while workers experience a fall in real income**, resulting in increased income inequality.

Inflation can also **widen the income gap between fixed and variable income earners**. In an economy, the high income earners tend to be variable income earners. This is because firm owners earn profits from businesses while top management earns huge bonuses, often pegged to profits or revenue. Therefore, **as the prices of goods and services rise, the incomes of variable income earners may increase in tandem**. Hence, **their incomes are somewhat protected against inflation, and they may even experience higher real incomes**.

However, for fixed income earners, **as prices of goods and services rise, their nominal incomes remain constant**. As such, their **purchasing power falls**. They are now able to purchase less with the same amount of income. This is made worse by the fact that **a large proportion of the population may be fixed income earners**. This means that **real incomes are redistributed from a large group of low income people and further concentrated into the hands of a few high-earning individuals**.

Since variable income earners may experience higher real income while fixed income earners experience a fall in real incomes, there is hence a **widening income gap between fixed income earners and variable income earners**.

Inflation, through the **disparity in bargaining power** of trade unions, can also result in income inequality. Strong unions are able to bargain for higher wages. Hence, **workers in strong unions should already have relatively higher wages**. On the other hand, workers in weak unions will have relatively lower wages. There is hence **existing income inequality** between workers in strong and weak unions. Due to inflation, workers in **strong unions are able to better protect themselves against inflation by bargaining successfully for higher wages since they have stronger bargaining power**. This ensures that their incomes preserve their real value. However, **workers in weaker trade unions and non-unionised workers will not be able to do so**. Furthermore, the bargaining for higher wages by workers in strong unions can spark off a **wage-price spiral, further decreasing the real incomes of other workers in weaker trade unions**. Income inequality is hence worsened.

Inflation also **widens the wealth gap between the wealthy and the poor**. The **wealthy tends to be fixed asset owners** and have their **wealth stored in fixed assets like gold and housing**. As the prices of goods and services increase, the value of these physical assets tends to increase. Hence, the **real value of wealth of these fixed asset owners tend to be protected against inflation**. On the other hand, the lower income earners do not have sufficient funds to purchase these fixed assets. Rather, if there is any income unspent, they will save in banks which offer no protection against rising inflation rates. For a given nominal savings rate, the real rate of return falls with inflation and may even be negative. Hence, while the real value of the wealth of the wealthy may be preserved, the real value of the wealth of the lower income earners will be eroded, thereby increasing wealth inequality.

22. Explain what the Balance of Payments consists of and what constitutes a healthy Balance of Payments.

The Balance of Payments (BOP) is an accounting statement that shows a country's economic transactions with the rest of the world over a specific period of time, usually a year. This includes transactions in goods and services, real assets, financial assets, income flows and transfers.

Every transaction is either a **credit or debit item**. It is a credit item if it results in an inflow of currencies as a receipt of payment and it is a debit item if it results in an outflow of currencies to make payments. The BOP comprises of 2 main accounts – the Current Account (CA) and the Capital and Financial Account (KFA).

The CA comprises of the **balance of trade (BOT), net income flows and net current transfers.** The BOT is the difference between the **export revenue earned (X) and the import expenditure spent (M).** Income flows refer to **investment income** in the form of rent, interest, profits, or dividends flowing into and out of the country. For example, with respect to Singapore's BOP, dividends or profits earned by a Singaporean owning shares or stocks in a company listed in the US is considered an inflow. Dividends or profits earned by a foreigner from owning stocks, bonds or shares in a company listed in Singapore are considered an outflow. Current transfers are **one way monetary transfers** that do not reap rewards. This can include government aid to other countries such as Singapore gifting about 16 million for reconstruction projects for tsunami-hit countries like Indonesia, Sri Lanka and the Maldives in 2005. It also includes foreign aid receipts from international organizations such as the World Bank and the remittances of foreign workers.

Tip

A CA Surplus or deficit is usually **caused by the balance of trade** since it is usually the **largest component** in the CA. Therefore, a CA surplus is usually the result of a trade surplus and the converse is also true.

The KFA records both long and short-term portfolio investments, foreign direct investments (FDI), debt forgiveness, migrant transfers and acquisition and disposal of non-financial assets like patents and copyrights. **FDI refers to the purchase and sale of real assets** like **manufacturing plants or acquiring existing firms**. It involves a foreign investor acquiring a **lasting interest and a large degree of influence or control over the management** of an enterprise located in one's economy. For example, Apple coming to Singapore to set up a research facility and office would be considered an FDI inflow into Singapore. **Long-term portfolio investments refer to the** purchase or sale of company shares and government bonds. Hot money flows refer to short-term monetary flows that occur to take advantage of **differences in countries' interest rates** and changes in exchange rates.

Generally, a healthy BOP is a BOP in equilibrium, whereby over the years, the BOP surpluses and deficits cancel each other out i.e. the credits equal to the debits. On the other hand, a BOP disequilibrium refers to a situation whereby there is **persistent BOP surplus or deficit.** However, what constitutes a healthy BOP tends to differ between countries. Small and Open Economies (SOEs) tend to favour a BOP surplus given their heavy reliance on exports and FDI for economic growth. Accumulating BOP surpluses also help them accumulate foreign exchange reserves in order to perform exchange rate interventions when needed. Exchange rate policy is usually a key policy for SOEs due to their dependence on trade. Moreover as SOEs also tend to be heavily reliant on imports due to a lack of natural resources, they also have a need to accumulate FOREX reserves to secure their ability to pay for imports in the future.

Larger and more developed economies may have BOP deficits due to outward FDI, but this will be met by a corresponding improvement in the BOP position in the long-run due to income inflows from profit repatriation, and may therefore not be a cause for concern.

A healthy BOP serves as an indicator of economic competitiveness. On the other hand, persistent deficits usually reflect a lack of competitiveness, which will eventually hurt economic growth and also result in macroeconomic instability such as a plunge in the exchange rate value and spike in imported inflation. If a healthy BOP is not achieved, a

BOP crisis can occur whereby the country can no longer pay for essential imports or service its foreign currency denominated debt.

23. Discuss the effects of a Balance of Payments surplus.

A BOP surplus can spur both actual and potential economic growth, reduce unemployment, reduce imported inflation, accelerate technological advancement and enable accumulation of FOREX reserves as security. However, it can also lead to increased retaliatory and inflationary pressures, as well as the Dutch Disease effect.

Assuming that the surplus is mainly due to a credit in the Current Account (CA) as a result of improving balance of trade (BOT) and profit repatriation from investments overseas, there is a **net inflow of money into the circular flow of income.** The rising net exports (X-M) due to an improving BOT leads to a rise in aggregate demand (AD). Via the multiplier effect, there will be a **multiplied increase in real GDP.** As firms increase derived demand for factors of production including labour in order to increase output, **unemployment also falls. Hence, a BOP surplus can spur economic growth and reduce unemployment.**

Assuming the surplus is mainly due to a credit in the Capital and Financial Account (KFA) as a result of increasing inflows of foreign direct investments (FDI), this can bring about **new technology** and **job opportunities**. It will have an **expansionary effect** on the economy as the increase in investments will increase AD, resulting in a multiplied increase in real GDP via the multiplier effect.

Furthermore, an increase in FDI inflows may also **increase the productive capacity of the economy** as foreign firms **set up production facilities and increase the amount of capital goods and level of technology in the economy.** Often, these foreign firms will bring with them **new technical know-how and** skills that can be transferred to the local labour force. This will therefore help increase the long-run aggregate supply (LRAS), increase potential growth, allowing for sustainable and non-inflationary economic growth.

A BOP surplus also means the foreigners are demanding more of the domestic currency. This would lead to an **appreciation of currency.** Hence, **imports will become cheaper** and this can help to **reduce imported inflation.** This can be **especially useful during economic restructuring** where massive amounts of new capital goods may need to be purchased. Since imports are now cheaper, greater quantities of these capital goods can now be imported. This can result in technological advancement, allowing her to restructure and move up the value chain more quickly.

A BOP surplus also suggests that the central bank will be able to accumulate FOREX reserves, needed for intervention in the currency market. For example, to defend against speculative attacks on its currency value, and to secure the economy's future ability to pay for imports.

However, a persistent BOP surplus could lead to an unstable situation because of increased retaliatory pressures. A surplus in one country necessarily implies a deficit for some others, and BOP deficits in other countries is unsustainable (see next chapter), possibly leading to increased protectionism in future as other countries in deficit retaliate against the country in surplus, possibly even escalating into a trade war. This will result in a fall in trade activity across the world, and all countries affected will suffer a fall in economic growth and standard of living.

Furthermore, a large Balance of Trade surplus could lead to increased inflationary pressures via **demand-pull inflation**. This happens if the productive capacity of the economy has not expanded sufficiently while there are continued injections into the circular flow of income. Due to the rising AD, an upward pressure on prices results as foreigners bid up prices, whilst a lack of spare capacity in the economy pushes firms to compete for the factors of production in order to produce more to meet the increasing demand, pushing up factor prices and hence leading to higher general price levels and demand-pull inflation.

A BOP surplus could also lead to the **Dutch Disease effect**. Assuming the BOP surplus is a result of large scale FDI inflows borne from the discovery of natural resources, usually to mine oil or other valuable commodities, the sudden influx of FDI inflows will result in a rapid appreciation in the exchange rate. As such, other export sectors will lose price competitiveness, dampening export revenue. If this persists, such export sectors may shrink as they are unable to compete and firms would have to shut down and relocate. This happened in Netherlands during the 1970s with discovery of a large natural gas field and subsequent decline of its manufacturing industries. It can lead to the economy's overdependence on natural resource based sectors, especially since such resources are finite.

Evaluation

Ultimately, whether a surplus leads to positive or negative consequences **depends largely on the cause of the surplus and the state of the economy**. If the surplus is due to improved economic competitiveness due to higher levels of productivity, long-term benefits of economic growth and low unemployment should follow. However, if it is due to an undervaluation of currency, just as China is often accused to be doing to help increase her export competitiveness, this may be perceived as unfair trade, eventually triggering retaliation which will harm the economy.

If the BOP surplus is due to massive hot money inflow, this will likely lead to demand-pull inflation and asset bubbles due to excessive money supply in the economy. Any boost to economic growth is likely to be short-lived as massive capital outflows are likely to occur in the future, producing detrimental effects such as the collapse of asset bubbles.

Moreover, if the economy is already near or at full employment level of output, then the BOP surplus will likely lead to overheating of the economy and demand-pull inflation. However, if there is a lot of spare capacity in the economy, then the economy could benefit from increased real national output and employment levels. Hence the effects of a BOP surplus do depend on the initial state of the economy.

Generally, surpluses are preferred over deficits since surpluses can spell both actual growth and potential growth. Actual growth can arise from an improvement in the BOT, leading to the increase in net exports and aggregate demand. Potential growth can arise from an improvement in the KFA, where an influx of FDI results in capital goods added to the economy and advancement in technology.

24. Discuss the effects of a Balance of Payments deficit.

A BOP deficit can hinder both actual and potential economic growth, result in imported inflation, exchange rate instability and ultimately in the long term reduce the standard of living.

A BOP deficit can lead to **negative economic growth**. Assuming the BOP deficit arises from deficit in the Current Account (CA) resulting from **worsening of the balance of trade (BOT)**, a **fall in net exports (X-M)** will **reduce the aggregate demand (AD), reducing real national income (RNY) by a multiplied amount via the reverse multiplier process.** Firms will reduce derived demand for factors of production including labour and this will result in increased unemployment. Furthermore, investments (I) may decrease as firms may be more pessimistic about the economy. Hence, while actual growth is reduced or turns negative, potential growth also falls due to the fall in the rate of capital accumulation.

The BOP deficit may mainly be due to a deficit in the Capital and Financial Account (KFA) resulting from **a fall in foreign direct investments (FDI) or increased direct investments abroad (DIA),** for example due to a **relocation of firms** towards lower cost economies. As a result, it can lead to **a fall in the level of investments and export revenue (due to firms' relocation), and thus a fall in the AD,** causing a multiplied fall in RNY through the reverse multiplier process. This **will likewise reduce the demand for labour and result in a rise in unemployment.** Furthermore, this can lead to a fall in the LRAS as the outflows would mean closing down of firms and manufacturing plants which will reduce the amount of capital goods and hence **reduce the productive capacity of the economy.**

Persistent deficits usually reflect a lack of competitiveness, which will eventually hurt economic growth and also result in macroeconomic instability such as a plunge in the exchange rate value and spike in imported inflation.

A BOP deficit suggests that foreigners are demanding less of the domestic currency, while locals may be increasing supply of domestic currency (in order to obtain foreign currencies). This would lead to a **depreciation of currency**. Hence, **imports will become**

more expensive and this can lead to **imported inflation**, resulting in domestic price instability and a fall in actual growth as the short-run aggregate supply (SRAS) falls.

The depreciation may also be perceived as a sign of weakness in the economy, triggering capital flight, which are portfolio and hot money outflows, causing a further depreciation of the currency and hence exchange rate instability.

If the central bank intervenes to prevent the depreciation, it would have to draw down on its FOREX reserves. This is because the central bank would need to sell its foreign reserves in order to buy domestic currency to increase or maintain its external value. The depletion of foreign reserves will likely lead to the collapse of the currency as the central bank will not be able to defend its currency against speculative attacks by currency traders. A BOP crisis would occur whereby the country can no longer pay for essential imports or service its foreign currency denominated debt.

Evaluation

However, A BOP deficit may not necessarily be a bad thing. These deficits could be mainly due to **temporary** CA deficits as a result of economic development requiring substantial imports of capital goods. Hence, the deficits can be reversed in the future, as the economy's productive capacity expands and begins to produce more and export more to the rest of the world. In the short term, if the country is importing a huge amount of goods and services, it is also a boost to material living standards. However, if the BOP deficit is persistent, this could be symptomatic of a larger, underlying problem like a lack of export competitiveness or lack of attractiveness to foreign firms, which will be harmful to a country's economic growth.

If the **size of the deficit** is small, a country can afford to fund these deficits with their foreign exchange reserves. However, if the size of the deficit is large as a proportion of the country's foreign exchange reserves, policies should be undertaken quickly to curb the BOP deficit.

Thus, BOP deficits are **especially harmful when they are persistent and large**.

A BOP deficit is also more worrying for Small and Open Economies (SOEs). SOEs usually heavily rely on imports for factor inputs due to a lack of natural resources. Persistent BOP deficits imply an inability to pay for these imports, and eventually either the economy will be overly indebted to foreigners, or its foreign exchange reserves will be depleted.

25. Explain the causes of a BOP deficit.

The Balance of Payments (BOP) is an accounting statement that shows a country's economic transactions with the rest of the world over a specific period of time, usually a year. This includes transactions in goods and services, real assets, financial assets, income flows and transfers.

Every transaction is either a **credit or debit item**. It is a credit item if it results in an inflow of currencies as a receipt of payment and it is a debit item if it results in an outflow of currencies to make payments. The BOP comprises of 2 main accounts – the Current Account (CA) and the Capital and Financial Account (KFA). The CA comprises of the **balance of trade (BOT), net income flows and net current transfers,** while the KFA records both long and short-term portfolio investments and foreign direct investments (FDI).

The loss in export price competitiveness can lead to a CA and BOP deficit. For example, USA has been experiencing CA deficits due to a loss of comparative advantage in many manufacturing sectors to developing economies such as China due to the latter's abundance of cheap labour. China has a **lower unit labour cost** especially in the manufacturing sector. This results in a **loss of price competitiveness of US exports. Assuming high degree of substitutability** between both countries' exports, US export earnings will decrease as other countries will choose to import from China instead. America's imports will also increase as their residents switch away from US produced goods and services to the relatively cheaper imports from China. Hence, there will be a fall in export revenue (X) coupled with a rise in import expenditure (M) resulting in a **large CA deficit.**

Furthermore, there may be a fall in FDI inflows into the US as firms are now keener to invest in other lower cost locations which will be more profitable for them. The emergence of economies like China and India bodes great long term economic growth prospects, which also serves to increase the expected rate of return on investments into these emerging economies. Falling FDI inflows may therefore lead to a **KFA deficit.** The large CA and KFA deficits therefore results in a BOP deficit.

CA and BOP deficits may also occur because trading partners undervalue their currencies. As the Chinese government keeps the Yuan undervalued by active intervention in the FOREX market, US will find Chinese goods cheaper in terms of the US dollar, while the Chinese will find that the US goods are more expensive in terms of Yuan. Quantity demanded for Chinese exports will rise while quantity demanded for US exports will fall. Assuming the Marshall-Lerner condition holds, where the sum of price elasticity of demand for exports and imports is greater than one i.e. $|PED_X + PED_M| > 1$, the trade balance will worsen and possibly leading to CA and BOP deficits.

Increasing affluence can lead to high import consumption, thereby resulting in a CA and BOP deficit. With strong economic growth, demand for imports may be increasing significantly, leading to an increase in M. A CA deficit may result especially if the domestic economy is growing faster than that of trading partners. Incomes of domestic consumers rise faster than the incomes of foreign consumers because of stronger economic growth domestically. As such, demand for imports is increasing faster than the demand for exports. Hence M may be increasing by a greater extent than X and the balance of trade may worsen leading to a CA and BOP deficit. In this situation, the rise in M will be especially significant if the imports consist mainly of luxury goods. Since demand for luxury goods are income elastic i.e. YED>1, any increase in incomes will lead to a more than proportionate increase in demand for imports. This hence results in a large increase M, hence more likely to result in a BOT deficit and hence, a CA and BOP deficit.

A relatively lower interest rate can also lead to a KFA and BOP deficit. If domestic interest rates fall relative to foreign interest rates, hot money investors will see a fall in their expected rate of return. As such, these investors would rather place their funds in other countries that they can earn higher returns. There will be a fall in hot money inflows as well as an increase in hot money outflows. This may lead to a KFA and BOP deficit.

Evaluation

Ultimately, it is imperative to ascertain the root cause of a BOP deficit. Some causes may be less of a concern given their temporary nature. For example, the massive import of capital goods due to early stages of industrialization. It is in fact beneficial for the economy as its productive capacity is expanding. Hence, a BOP deficit may not necessarily be detrimental.

However, if the BOP deficit is persistent, this could be symptomatic of a larger, underlying problem like a loss of export competitiveness or a lack of attractiveness to foreign firms, which will be harmful to a country's economic growth.

26. Explain what the Capital and Financial Account comprises of.

The Capital and Financial Account (KFA) consists of international transactions mainly involving the acquisition and sale of financial and real assets. Foreign direct investments (FDI) and short and long-term portfolio investments comprise of the majority of the KFA.

FDIs refer to investments made by a company or entity based in one country into a company or entity based in another country. These require the investor, which is usually an MNC, to acquire a **long-term and significant interest** in the company they invested upon, involving the foreign ownership of domestic physical assets such as land and property. This can be achieved by **setting up a subsidiary company** in the foreign country or by either **acquiring shares** of an existing overseas company or through a **merger** with an existing overseas company. For Example, if Apple wants to set up a manufacturing plant in Singapore to create their new A9 microchips, it can set up a new firm Apple Singapore, or buy out 51% of Creative's shares in order to take ownership of Creative and use their resources to begin manufacturing of these new A9 microchips. All these would constitute an inward FDI into Singapore.

Long-term portfolio investments refer to investments in financial assets like stocks, shares and bonds. It is an investment made with **the expectation of earning a return in the long-term**. It differs from FDI which requires the investor to take a large stake in a company and in many instances be involved with its daily operations. Examples of long-term portfolio investments include purchases of stocks and shares, government bonds, corporate bonds, and real estate investment.

Short-term portfolio investments are **typically over a short period of time**, and include hot money investments, mainly in the form of bank deposits to take advantage of high interest rates and favourable changes in the exchange rates.

27. Explain possible causes for deterioration of the Capital and Financial Account.

The Capital and Financial Account (KFA) is a **record of all international transactions involving the sale and acquisitions of financial and real assets between the country and the rest of the world within a fixed time period, usually one yea**r. It consists mainly of both long and short-term **portfolio investments** as well as **foreign direct investments (FDI)**. Portfolio investments comprise **of short-term portfolio investments like hot money and long-term portfolio investments in stocks, shares and bonds**. FDIs refer to the setting up, acquiring or expansion of firms, which are usually MNCs, in the domestic economy.

Deterioration in the KFA can be brought about by a greater increase in outflows over inflows, or a greater decrease in inflows over outflows. One possible cause for the deterioration of the KFA is a **fall in the Marginal Efficiency of Investments (MEI)** in the country. The determinants of MEI include business confidence, political stability, availability of modern infrastructure, tax rates, and level of labour productivity. A fall in business confidence, loss of political stability or lack of corporate infrastructure, increase in corporate taxes, and an increase in unit labour costs could result in a fall in MEI, which is the expected rate of return on investments in the country. This will result in a **fall in FDI inflows** as foreign firms will rather invest in other countries that are able to yield them higher rates of return. It also cause **more outflows, known as direct investments abroad (DIA),** as local firms may relocate to other countries where they could earn higher profits.

Additionally, a **lower interest rate** relative to other countries will result in increased **hot money outflows and reduce hot money inflows** which will cause a deterioration in the KFA. An **expectation that the exchange rate will depreciate** could result in increased **hot money outflows and a decrease in hot money inflows** as investors no longer want to hold on to assets denominated in the currency that will soon be worth less. Foreign investors may close their overseas bank accounts and transfer their funds back home before the depreciation, thereby leading to hot money outflows and hence a deterioration in the KFA. Similarly, foreign hot money investors may also be deterred from investing, resulting in a fall in hot money inflows. Furthermore, this may also cause foreign firms to stay out as an impending depreciation creates uncertainty and reduces the rate of return since profits when converted to home currency and repatriated back home will now be worth less should there be a depreciation.

A **recession** could result in a **fall in demand for stocks, shares and bonds** of domestic firms as **sentiments are poor** and investors do not expect these firms to do well. Hence, there will be an **increase in outflows and a decrease in inflows** as local investors and foreign investors withdraw their investments from the country and invest in other countries instead.

Evaluation

However, a deterioration in the KFA may not necessarily be due to unfavourable factors. It could be caused by the **growth and expansion of local firms**. Over time, these firms could have obtained the necessary resources to expand and internationalize. It is therefore natural for these firms to expand into overseas markets to increase revenue or to capitalize on greater cost advantages through reaping internal economies of scale or through international vertical specialization. In this situation, these firms may cause a KFA deterioration through increasing DIAs. However, these DIAs are likely to result in current account (CA) inflows in the future due to the repatriation of profits which will be reflected as an increase in income inflows. Hence, the overall BOP can remain healthy in the long run.

It is therefore important to ascertain the causes of deterioration in order to determine whether or how a government should intervene. For example, causes like a fall in relative interest rates may not be of serious concern and are usually temporary in nature. This means that the KFA may easily improve in the future. An expansion of local firms overseas can also be highly beneficial to the domestic economy since it contributes to increasing the real GNP. However, factors leading to unfavourable expected rates of return for foreign firms can lead to a long-term deterioration of the KFA if uncorrected, and reduces actual and potential economic growth.

28. Explain the J-Curve Effect.

The J-curve shows that a **depreciation of the currency may initially lead to deterioration in the balance of trade (BOT)** before **showing an improvement.**

**Trade Balance
(X-M)**

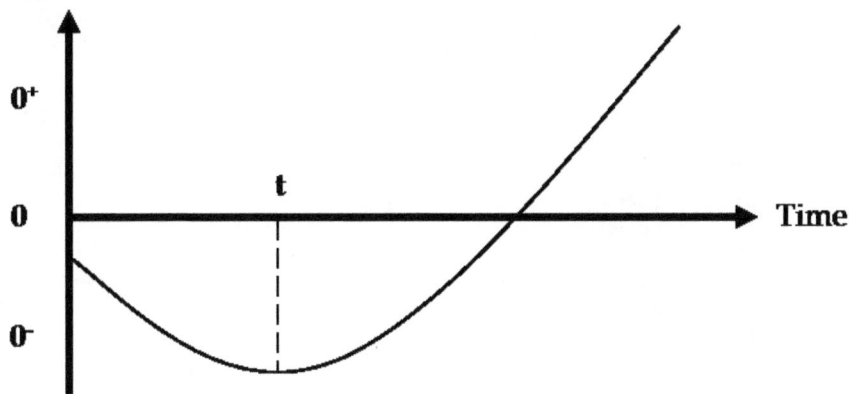

Fig 1: J-Curve Effect

A government may pursue a depreciation of the currency in order to correct a BOT deficit. A depreciation would make exports cheaper in terms of foreign currency, and imports more expensive in terms of domestic currency. Instead, it may lead to **an initial deterioration** of the trade balance. This happens when the Marshall Lerner's condition, i.e. $|PED_x + PED_m| > 1$, is not met. This occurs when **demand for imports and exports are highly price-inelastic in the short-term** usually due to the existence of contractual agreements between importers and exporters and the lack of time for consumers to source for suitable substitutes. Empirically, this usually happens during the first 6 months following the depreciation, making t in Fig 1 a time period of 6 months.

In the **long-term**, beyond time t in Fig 1, domestic consumers would have found cheaper domestic substitutes and some producers would have completed their contractual obligations. They are hence able to switch to domestic substitutes, resulting in a more price elastic demand for imports. Similarly, foreigners are now more able to switch to the cheaper exports as **contractual obligations with other suppliers are completed**. This results in a more price elastic demand for exports. At this point, the Marshall Lerner's Condition is met. Hence, the **trade balance improves thereafter**, to the point where it **surpasses the initial trade balance** and now the economy may even enjoy a trade surplus.

29. Explain 3 examples of conflicts in macroeconomic goals.

The 5 macroeconomic goals are sustained economic growth, full employment, low and stable inflation, healthy Balance of Payments (BOP) and a low degree of income inequality. Sometimes, conflicts in macro goals can occur, where **pursuing the fulfilment of one macro goal leads to the deterioration of another goal.**

Conflict 1: Pursuing Actual Economic Growth vs. Low Inflation

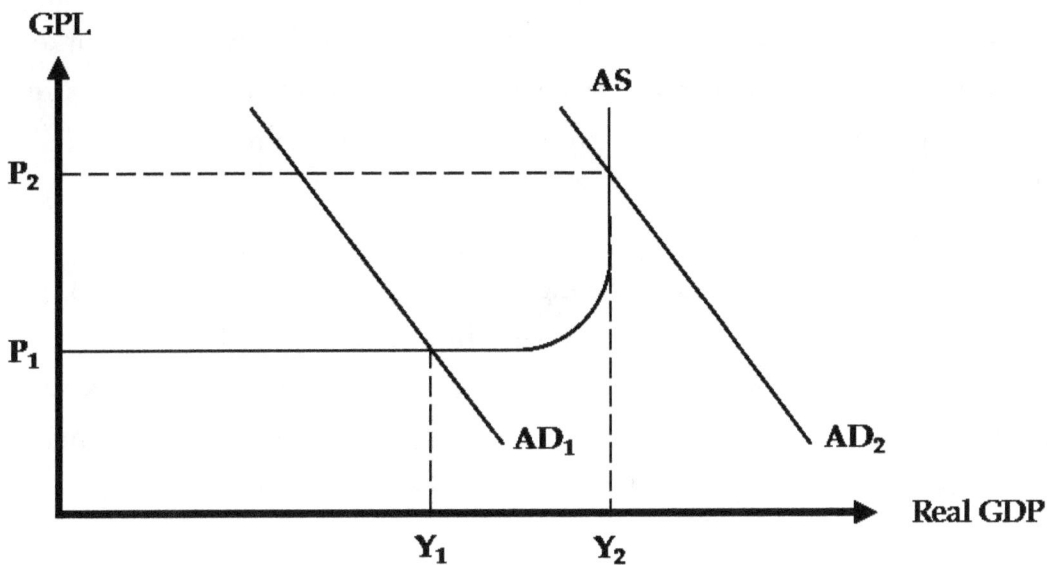

Fig 1: Actual Growth vs Low Inflation

As economies pursue economic growth via either expansionary fiscal or monetary policy, this will increase aggregate demand (AD) from AD_1 to AD_2 in Fig 1. As AD increases, quantity demanded of goods and services will exceed quantity supplied, resulting in a shortage and the bidding up prices. In response to higher prices and an unplanned decline in inventories, firms will increase production and hire more workers, thereby leading to increased real national output from Y_1 to Y_2 as well as higher employment levels. However, as firms increase production and hire more workers, there will be less spare capacity in the economy. Firms will begin to compete for resources and bid up prices for factors of production. They may pay workers higher wages and pay higher prices for raw materials. Hence, the unit cost of production will increase. This increase in cost will be passed on to consumers, contributing to an increase in general price levels (GPL) from P_1 to P_2. Hence, **high inflation rates may occur as economic growth is achieved.**

Conversely, in trying to reduce inflation rates, the government could pursue a contractionary monetary or fiscal policy. This will cause AD to fall from AD_2 to AD_1. As AD falls, firms will experience an unplanned increase in stocks and reduce production. Since firms produce less and now require fewer factor inputs, competition for these inputs will lessen and prices of these inputs will fall. This will eventually result in lower costs of production and hence contribute to the fall in GPL from P_2 to P_1. However, because firms cut back on production, total real national output is reduced and workers are laid off, causing the economy to contract from Y_2 to Y_1. Hence, the **lowered inflation rate is achieved at the expense of economic growth and full employment.**

Conflict 2: Pursuing Economic Growth vs. Low Degree of Income Inequality

In pursuing economic growth (especially through an export-led growth strategy), the economy may **undergo restructuring** whereby **certain industries will expand while others will decline**. As such, this will result in a **higher demand for workers who possess skills in the booming industries with comparative advantage**, while demand for workers in industries with comparative disadvantage will decrease.

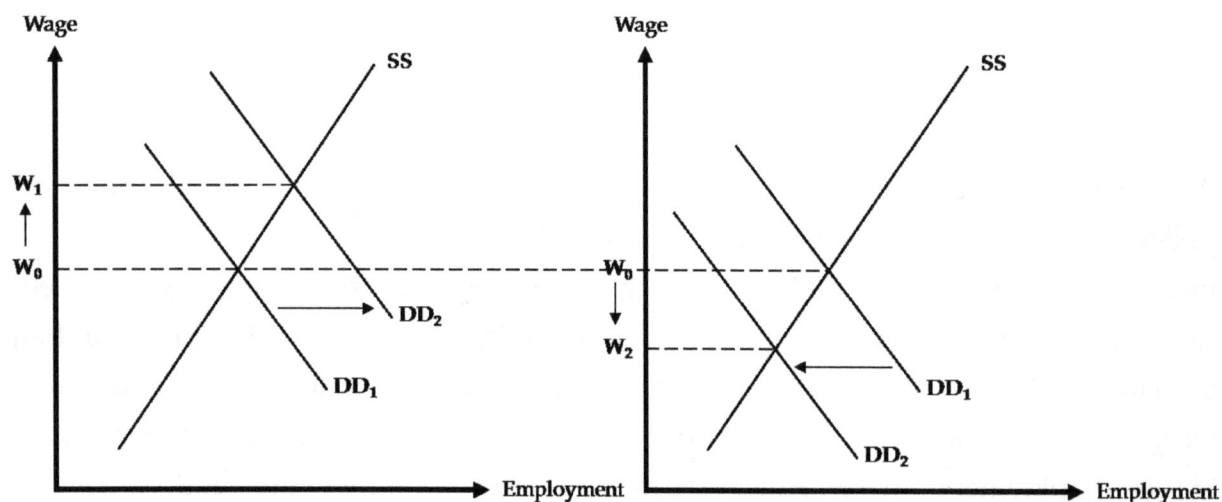

Fig 2: Expanding Industry Labour Market   Fig 3: Declining Industry Labour Market

Assume that initially, both industries offer similar wages at W_0 in Figs 2 and 3. However, in pursuing economic growth, there is an **increase in demand for workers who possess the skills to work in the expanding industry** from DD_1 to DD_2 in Fig 2. As demand increases, this exerts an upwards pressure on wages to increase from W_0 to W_1. In declining industries, demand for workers falls from DD_1 to DD_2 in Fig 3, and this will exert a downward pressure on wages, causing wages to decrease from W_0 to W_2.

Hence, workers in expanding industries earn higher wages while workers in declining industries receive lower wages. At the same time, structural unemployment may also occur as workers that are laid off in the declining industry do not possess the skills to begin working in the expanding industry. As such, **income inequality and structural unemployment occurs while economic growth is achieved.**

Furthermore, because economic growth leads to possible demand-pull inflation, it could also worsen income inequality between fixed income and variable income earners. In an economy, many high income earners tend to be variable income earners. This is because firm owners are among the high income earners and earn profits from their businesses while top management usually earn huge bonuses that are pegged to firm revenue or profits. Therefore, as the prices of goods and services rise, the **incomes of variable income earners tend to increase as well.** Hence, **the incomes of variable income earners are protected against inflation, and they may even experience higher real incomes.** However, **fixed income earners will definitely experience falling real incomes as** prices of goods and services rise. As such, their **purchasing power falls.** They are now able to purchase less with the same salaries.

This is made worse by the fact that **a large proportion of the population may be fixed income earners.** This means that **real incomes are redistributed from a large group of low income people and further concentrating it in the hands of a few high-earning individuals.**

Conflict 3: Pursuing Economic Growth vs. Balance of Payments Equilibrium
As **economies experience actual economic growth, real national income rises.** Because of the rise in incomes, purchasing power increases and demand for normal goods and services increases, including imports, resulting in an increase in import expenditure

(M). This is especially significant for imported luxury goods given that the demand for luxury goods is income elastic. As incomes increases, the demand for luxury imports will increase more than proportionately. As such, if the bulk of imports are luxury goods, M will increase very significantly as an economy undergoes economic growth. Due to this increase in M, the Balance of Trade (BOT) may deteriorate and incur a deficit. This can further lead to a Balance of Payments (BOP) deficit if this deficit is not met by an increase in capital inflows. Hence, the **BOP position may deteriorate as economic growth is achieved**.

Evaluation

Due to the presence of conflicts in macroeconomic goals, there is a need to be aware of Tinbergen's principle when implementing macroeconomic policies. The Tinbergen's principle states that for every macroeconomic problem, there needs to be at least one corresponding macroeconomic policy targeted specifically at solving the problem. For example, if the government is trying to achieve 3 macroeconomic goals, it needs at least 3 different policies.

There is also a need to weigh the relative magnitude of the various macroeconomic problems and degree of urgency. More urgent problems that would have massive short-term implications like massive unemployment should be addressed first and foremost, while other policies that address underlying structural issues can be undertaken when the immediate economic crisis has been averted.

Despite the conflicts, however, pursuing one goal often results in the fulfilment of another. For example, pursuing economic growth will most likely reduce unemployment, bringing the economy closer to full employment.

30. Explain how fiscal policies can reduce cyclical unemployment.

Fiscal policy can be classified into two forms; discretionary and non-discretionary fiscal policy. **Discretionary fiscal policy** involves the deliberate use of **government spending** and **taxation** to **influence economic activity** in a country. Non-discretionary fiscal policy involves **automatic fiscal stabilizers** like **unemployment benefits** and **progressive income taxes** to reduce the extent of a recession or overheating economy.

Cyclical unemployment refers to unemployment that arises due to **insufficient aggregate demand (AD)**. It is a situation where **AD is too low** to fully employ the available resources in the economy.

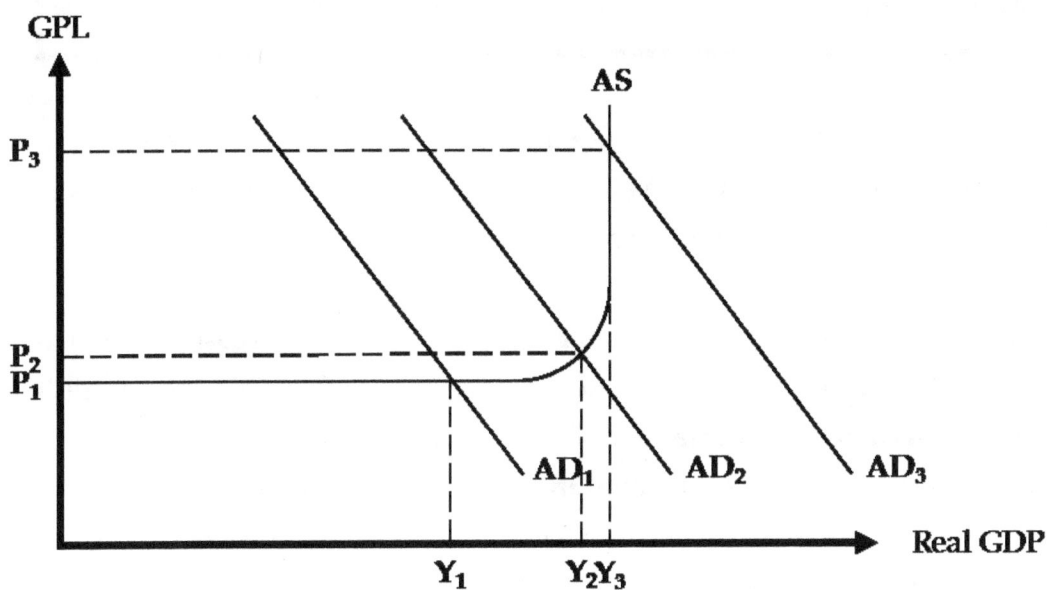

Fig 1: Fiscal Policy

Assuming the economy was initially in a recession, AD is low at AD_1 and it is operating along the Keynesian range at real output level of Y_1. This level of output is very far from the full employment level of output of Y_3, hence a high rate of cyclical unemployment.

Expansionary fiscal policy consists mainly of **increasing G** by raising government spending for development projects, as well as lowering T by **lowering personal and corporate income taxes.** Expansionary fiscal policy can also include increasing welfare payments, also referred to as transfer payments, to households.

By **reducing personal income taxes** and **increase transfer payments** to households, households' disposable income and purchasing power are increased, increasing their demand for goods and services and hence **increasing their level of consumption (C)**.

Note: While welfare payments involve government spending, it does not increase "G" in AD. Rather, it works by increasing "C". This is because there is no reciprocal good or service provided unlike, say, the spending on public works. The transfer payments increase household disposable income which in turn increases their purchasing power and hence consumption.

Reducing **corporate tax rates** will increase the after-tax profits of firms, increasing the expected rate of return on investment projects and hence, more investment projects will now be profitable. This leads to an increase in the level of investments (I).

The corresponding increases in G, I and C **thereby results in an increase in AD** from AD_1 to AD_2 in Fig 1, leading to a multiplied increase in real GDP via the multiplier effect. Firms will **experience an unplanned decrease in stocks and inventories**, and hence **hire more workers to increase the amount of output**. This will reduce the rate of cyclical unemployment. As real GDP increases towards Y_2, the economy also approaches full employment level Y_3, where there is zero cyclical unemployment.

Additionally, **non-discretionary fiscal policies** like unemployment benefits act as automatic stabilisers to **reduce the impact of a recession**. Referring to Fig 1, assume that the economy is initially operating at AD_3 and producing at Y_3. Due to a sudden world-wide economic downturn, the economy therefore experiences a fall in export revenue, resulting in a fall in net exports. This therefore leads to a severe fall in AD from AD_3 to AD_1, resulting in a massive fall in real output from Y_3 to Y_1. There is drastic massive negative economic growth and unemployment. However, due to unemployment benefits, households that experienced a loss of jobs are cushioned from the recession. They still enjoy certain levels of disposable income due to these unemployment benefits. Hence, this exerts an expansionary effect on the economy, resulting in a **lower fall in AD** from AD₃ to AD₂ as opposed to a fall from AD₃ to AD₂. Real GDP falls by a lesser extent from Y_3 to Y_2 and cyclical unemployment is, as a result, also less severe.

Evaluation

However, the **effectiveness depends on the nature of the industries** that are expanding. If the industries expanding output are capital intensive, the rise in AD and subsequent increase in production may increase the utilization of capital goods without much corresponding increase in labour utilization. Hence, a high rate of cyclical unemployment may still exist. In contrast, if industries are mainly labour-intensive, any increase in production will result in more significant fall in cyclical unemployment.

Furthermore, fiscal policy takes time to come into full effect. The time lag could be, for example, administrative in nature, given that time is required between recognition of the need for fiscal policy, and the planning, designing and signing of policies and contracts in order to enact the fiscal policy. Such **time lag** can lead to a whole host of other problems. For example, if an economy was already recovering, **by the time the fiscal policy comes into full effect,** it may cause the economy to overheat and experience demand-pull inflation.

Countries with a **small multiplier** will experience a **smaller increase in real national output** despite the same initial injection, making the expansionary fiscal policy less effective. Such countries include the small and open economies (SOEs) that have a have a greater dependence on imported goods and services. Hence, they tend to have a higher Marginal Propensity to Withdraw (MPW) due to higher Marginal Propensity to Import. The higher the MPW, the lower the size of the multiplier, reducing the effectiveness.

SOEs may **also find** the exchange rate policy to be more effective in increasing AD. This is because SOEs are usually dependent on exports for growth, since they usually have a very small domestic market. Expansionary fiscal policy is only able to stimulate domestic demand, which is limited, whereas exchange rate policy can stimulate external demand.

Finally, the government may have had to borrow from the private sector in order to fund the expansionary fiscal policy. This leads to a fall in supply of loanable funds, because savings fall as the public purchases more government bonds, increasing interest rates, which results in a higher cost of borrowing, discouraging C and I. **The expansionary fiscal policy is said to have crowded out private spending and AD may not increase as much as expected from the fiscal policy due to a fall in C and I arising from the higher interest rates.**

Tip It is imperative to note that this does not mean fiscal policies are completely useless in countries with a small multiplier. These policies still work, but they are just less effective as compared to the case of an economy with a large multiplier.

31. Explain how a progressive income tax system can help to decrease income inequality.

Progressive income tax is a **direct, ad-valorem** tax levied upon the income of taxpayers, where taxpayers **face a higher marginal tax rate as their income increases.** Direct taxes are such that the impact of the tax and incidence of the tax are borne by the same person. In an **ad-valorem income tax**, taxes are based on a certain percentage of total income, as opposed to a specific tax which levies a fixed amount of tax independent of income level.

Progressive income taxes **tax more heavily on the income of the rich** and **taxes less heavily on the income of the poor**. The higher income earners will pay a larger proportion of their income in taxes while the lower income earners will pay a lower **proportion of their income in taxes.** Hence, the gap between their disposable **incomes becomes smaller**, decreasing the income inequality.

For example, David earns $100,000 annually and Andrew earns $20,000 annually. Under a progressive tax system, the 1st 50,000 earned is taxed at 10%, while the next 50,000 is taxed at 15%. Therefore, Andrew pays $20,000 x 0.1 = $2,000 in taxes while David pays $50,000 x 0.1 + $50,000 x 0.15 = $12,500. Hence, David pays a larger proportion of his income in taxes (12.5%) as compared to Andrew (10%). This leaves David with $87,500 disposable income and Andrew with $18 000 disposable income. Initially, the difference between David and Andrew's income was $80 000. After the tax however, the difference narrows to $69 500. Hence, income inequality is reduced.

Furthermore, the greater tax revenue obtained from the rich allows the government to **further provide welfare benefits** by giving out welfare payments, subsidizing healthcare, education and other basic necessities for the poor. This further narrows the income gap between the rich and the poor, thereby improving equity and ensuring that the lower income earners have access to basic necessities and merit goods.

Progressive income taxes are also **automatic fiscal stabilizers**. As an economy enters a recession, real national income falls. This means that households are earning less. As such, they will also be charged at a lower marginal tax rate than before. This has a cushioning effect on their disposable incomes, and helps to stabilize consumption levels, **cushion against an economic downturn**.

Conversely, as an economy experiences rapid growth, real national income rises and this means that households are earning more. The marginal tax rate that households face will hence increase. This serves to reduce the increase in disposable income, slowdown the increase in consumption, thereby reducing the rate of economic growth to **prevent overheating and inflation**.

32. Explain how the Central Bank increases and decreases interest rates.

The Central Bank can **increase interest rates (i/r)** by **decreasing money supply in the economy**. This is achieved by issuing government bonds that give a fixed return on capital. As bonds are issued, commercial banks and the general public purchase these bonds and less funds will be saved in the commercial banks. This will reduce the supply of loanable funds from SS_1 to SS_2, leading to a shortage which exerts an upward pressure on the price of loans. Therefore, the i/r increases from i_1 to i_2.

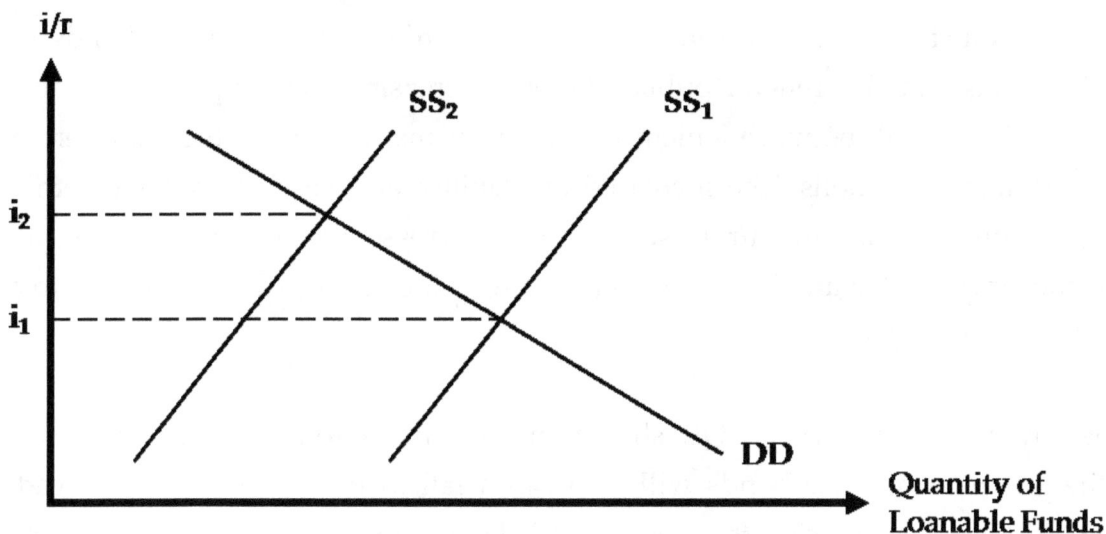

Fig 1: Demand and Supply of Loanable Funds

Conversely, the Central Bank **decreases i/r by increasing money supply** in the economy. This is achieved by the Central Bank buying government bonds from the private sector. As more bonds are purchased from the private sector, more money is in the hands of commercial banks and the general public. This increases the supply of loanable funds from SS_2 to SS_1. At the prevailing market rate of i_2, leading to a surplus which exerts downward pressure on the price of loans. Therefore, the i/r decreases from i_2 to i_1.

33. Explain quantitative easing.

Quantitative easing (QE) is a government policy option where the Central Bank **increases money supply** to **decrease interest rates (i/r)** in order to **stimulate economic activity**. This is achieved by purchasing assets from the private sector on a large scale. QE tends to be undertaken when i/r is already very low and repeated efforts at expansionary fiscal and monetary policies have failed to stimulate economic growth.

As the government undertakes QE, the Central Bank will purchase long-term bonds on a large scale from the private sector. This will place more money in the hands of commercial banks and the general public, thereby increasing the supply of loanable funds. Hence, banks will be more lenient in making loans, extending the loan period and lowering loan conditions. The increased availability and ease of credit, together with further cuts in long-term i/r is supposed to increase the amount of loans to stimulate consumption (C) and investments (I), thereby increasing AD and leading to a rise in real national output.

When the government undertakes QE, short-term i/r is likely to already be close to 0. Hence, the purchase of these bonds will result in a fall in the long-term i/r instead. Investors will take this as a sign that the Central Bank is looking to depress i/r in the long-run. I will therefore increase, increasing AD and real output.

Evaluation

Excessive Leakages
The increased money supply need not be retained in the economy. Majority of the funds may be leaked out of the economy and invested overseas, especially when confidence in this economy is still poor. For example, these investments can take the form of hot money outflows seeking to earn higher i/r in other economies. In that case, the QE policy will not be effective in stimulating C and I in the domestic economy. Furthermore, even if consumption were to increase, it could be mainly on imported goods and services instead, which would not contribute to boosting the domestic economy.

Positive Effect on Net Exports

Nevertheless, the QE policy can lead to a positive side effect of depreciation in the exchange rate (e/r). This arises from massive hot money outflows as explained earlier, which would increase the supply of domestic currency in the foreign exchange market in order for hot money investors to obtain foreign currencies by trading in domestic currency, leading to a fall in the external value of the currency. Prices of exports in terms of foreign currencies will fall and prices of imports in terms of domestic currency will rise. More exports would be sold as the quantity demanded for exports increases, while fewer imports would be purchased as quantity demanded for imports fall and consumers switch to domestically produced substitutes. This would lead to an increase in export revenue (X) and a fall in import expenditure (M), increasing the net exports (X-M), resulting in an increase in AD and real output. This is arguably how QE had worked for the US in recent years.

Problematic End to QE

Furthermore, there is a fear that when the Central Bank starts to sell all the government bonds it has accumulated during QE, interest rates will start soaring, thereby deterring consumption and investments and hurting economic growth. For example, when the US FED suggested QE tapering in 2014, interest rates around the world started to increase, due to fear of massive hot money outflows back to the US, which can lead to various problems including exchange rate instability and bursting of asset bubbles.

34. Explain the crowding out effect.

In order to undertake expansionary fiscal policy, governments may have to incur budget deficits which may require them to borrow from the public. Crowding out effect refers to the situation whereby the **government's borrowing** from the public leads to **higher interest rates** which **reduces private investment spending, hence reducing aggregate demand (AD).**

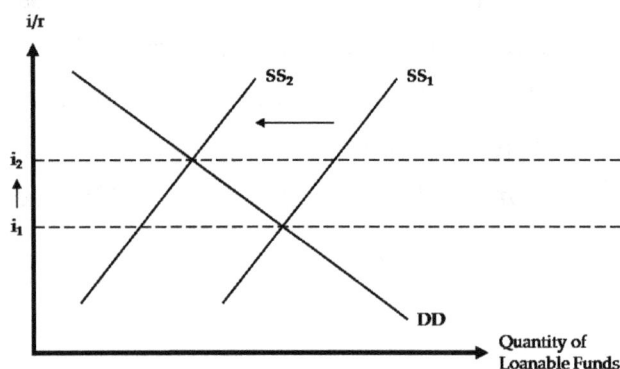

Fig 1: Demand and Supply of Loanable Funds

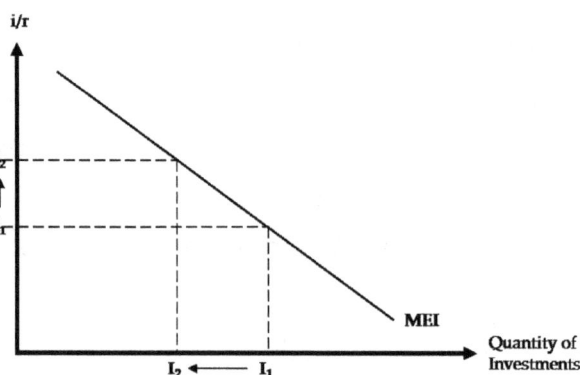

Fig 2: Marginal Efficiency of Investment

Government's borrowing is often done by **issuing bonds** to the public that pay a fixed amount of interest over a certain time period. As the public buys these bonds, the amount of savings deposited in banks will shrink since households have used their savings to purchase the government bonds. This leads to a fall in the supply of loanable funds from SS_1 to SS_2 in Fig 1 and an increase in **interest rates from i_1 to i_2. This will mean that the cost of borrowing has increased and** certain investments that were profitable at lower interest rates will no longer be profitable. Hence, the amount of investments by the private sector will fall from I_1 to I_2 in Fig 2. The investments have thus been "**crowded out**" by government borrowing.

For economies with free capital flows, crowding out can also occur through the higher interest rates attracting more hot money inflows. These hot money inflows will cause an appreciation of the exchange rate, which will result in a loss of export price competitiveness, "crowding out" exports.

GPL

AS

P₃

P₁

AD₁ AD₂ AD₃

Real GDP

Y₁ Y₂ Y₃

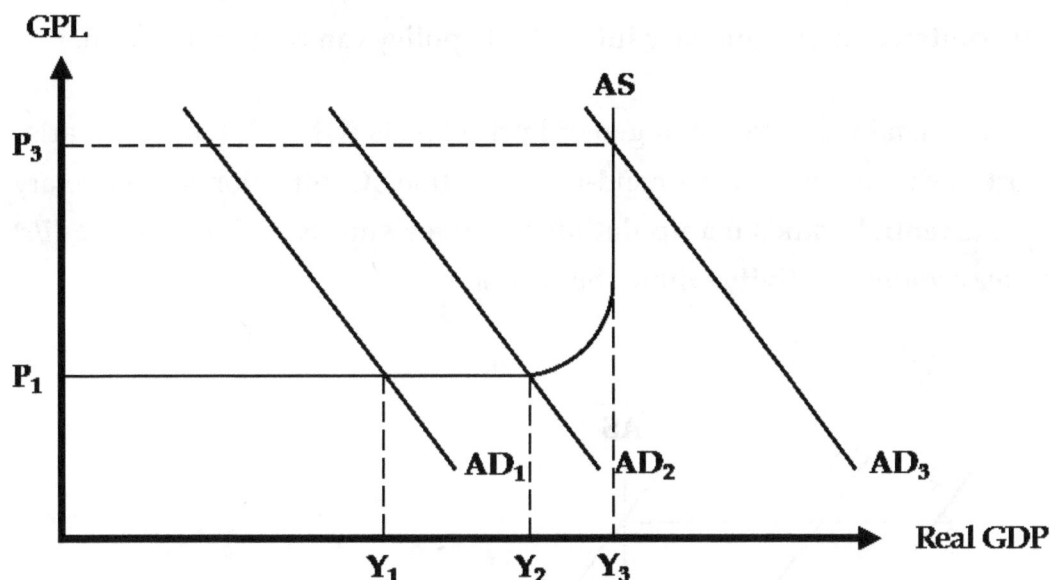

Fig 3: Crowding Out Effect

As a government undertakes expansionary fiscal policy, AD increases from AD_1 to AD_3 in Fig 3 as additional spending leads to greater levels of production by firms and greater utilization of factors of production, leading to a multiplied increase in real GDP from Y_1 to Y_3. However, due to the crowding out effect, the resulting fall in investments and/or exports lead to a fall in AD from AD_3 to AD_2. The effectiveness of expansionary fiscal policy is hence **muted by the crowding out effect**, with real GDP only increasing from Y_1 to Y_2 rather than to Y_3.

Evaluation

However, countries like Singapore that have substantial national reserves are unlikely to experience the crowding-out effect, since they will not need to resort to borrowing to finance expansionary fiscal policies.

35. Explain how contractionary monetary interest rate policy can reduce inflation.

Inflation refers to a **sustained increase in general price levels (GPL)**. Inflation can arise from either cost-push inflation or demand-pull inflation. Contractionary monetary policy refers to the **central bank's manipulation of money supply or interest rate (i/r)** in order to **reduce economic activity** within the economy.

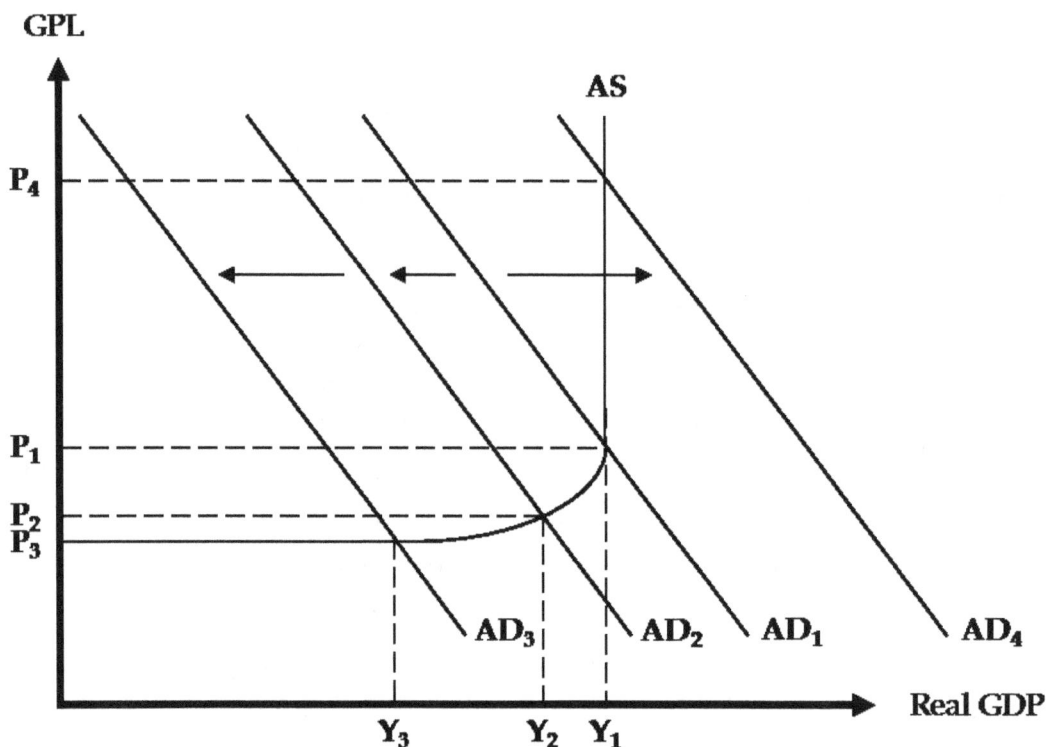

GPL

(graph showing AS curve, AD curves AD_1, AD_2, AD_3, AD_4, price levels P_1, P_2, P_3, P_4, and real GDP levels Y_1, Y_2, Y_3; arrows pointing left and right)

Real GDP

Fig 1: Contractionary Monetary Policy

Assume that initially, the economy is expected to experience demand-pull inflation as aggregate demand (AD) increases from AD_1 to AD_4, resulting in a rise in general price levels (GPL) from P_1 to P_4 without any increase in real GDP.

In order to reduce inflation, the central bank can contract the money supply, causing i/r to rise. As **i/r rises**, the cost of borrowing increases. The opportunity cost of consumption also increases given that a higher rate of return on savings is forgone. This **deters consumption (C)** and consumers will purchase fewer big-ticket items, such as cars, that require loans since the financing of these purchases is now more expensive. Furthermore, **investments (I) will fall** as cost of borrowing has increased and fewer investment projects are now profitable. The fall in consumption and investments leads to a **fall in AD** from AD_1 to AD_2. Because AD has fallen, firms will face an unplanned increase in stocks and inventories. Firms will hence **reduce production** and there will also be a downward pressure on prices to clear excess supply, contributing to a fall in GPL from P_1 to P_2. **Real GDP will fall more than proportionately to the initial fall in C and I via the reverse multiplier effect from Y_1 to Y_2.** As firms reduce production and lay off workers, **cyclical unemployment** will increase. With real GDP and more spare capacity in the economy, competition for factors of production including labour is no longer as intense as before and hence, **wages as well as other factor prices fall.** This results in a **fall in unit costs of production, thereby contributing to the fall in GPL** from P_1 to P_2.

Evaluation

Conflicts in Macroeconomic Goals

However, using contractionary monetary policy can possibly cause a **"hard landing"**, where AD decreases to such an extent that it **causes a recession**. This can lead to significantly higher unemployment rates. Referring to the diagram, contractionary monetary policy could result in a fall in AD from AD_1 all the way to AD_3, resulting in a small fall in GPL from P_1 to P_3 and a much larger fall in real GDP from Y_1 to Y_3. Hence, it is a policy that is best undertaken only if the economy is operating high up on the classical range, where the economy has been experiencing high rates of demand-pull inflation i.e. when the economy is already at AD_4. This could effect a fall in AD from AD_4 to AD_1 with a fall in GPL from P_4 to P_1, without any corresponding fall in real GDP. Should the contractionary monetary policy also result in hot money inflows, this will cause an unplanned appreciation of the exchange rate, worsening the Balance of Trade and Balance of Payments.

Interest-rate Elasticity of Consumption and Investments

The effectiveness of contractionary monetary policy **depends on how sensitive C and I are to an increase in i/r.** If the demand for C and I is i/r inelastic, C and I will not decrease by much despite an increase in i/r. For example, in Singapore, majority of I is due to FDI, and these FDI are not influenced by domestic i/r given that they have their own source of funds. They will hence not be affected by an increase in the cost of borrowing in Singapore. Hence the demand for investments in Singapore is likely to be i/r inelastic.

In addition, during times of extreme optimism for example due to strong growth prospects, firms may also be highly unresponsive to the increase in interest rates and therefore the level of investments fall less than proportionately to the increase in interest rates.

Fall in Potential Growth Rate

As contractionary monetary policy **discourages I**, this will lead to a **fall in the rate of capital accumulation and hence potential growth**. Yet, potential growth is necessary to help avoid demand-pull inflation and allow for sustainable non-inflationary economic growth. By inhibiting potential growth, demand-pull inflation could arise again in the future as growth in AD outpaces growth in long-run aggregate supply (LRAS).

Root Cause of the Problem

In addition, we also have to examine the cause of inflation. Should it be **cost-push instead of demand-pull, contractionary monetary policy will not solve the root cause**. It can only provide a temporary respite against the rising price levels. Furthermore, **if the economy is operating in the Keynesian range, contractionary monetary policy will have no impact on price levels**. Supply-side policies such as to increase labour productivity or direct controls over prices and wages may have to be undertaken instead to combat against the cost-push inflation.

36. Explain fiscal austerity.

Fiscal austerity refers to a situation where the government decides to **aggressively reduce spending and increase tax revenues over a certain number of years**, due to **excessive government debt** resulting in problems repaying the debt. This is a result of persistent budget deficits - government expenditure consistently exceeding tax revenues over many years. Often, creditors may impose austerity conditions as part of a debt restructuring exercise.

The government can reduce expenditure by cutting welfare payments, reducing subsidies, cancelling or postponing public work projects and cutting civil service salaries etc. Governments will also seek to raise tax revenues by imposing new taxes such as the carbon tax on fossil fuels that France recently implemented, increasing tax rates and more seriously enforcing against tax evasion. A prime example of fiscal austerity being undertaken is in Greece, where massive government debt has forced the government into fiscal austerity in a bid to reduce debt that has spiralled upwards to 175% of GDP.

Fiscal austerity exerts a **contractionary effect on the economy**. The reduction in government expenditure (G) and increasing of taxes, for example personal income taxes, reduces the amount of disposable income that consumers have, decreasing consumption (C). Increasing indirect taxes will also reduce C. As a result, **aggregate demand (AD)** falls which leads to **reduced economic growth and greater unemployment**. Furthermore, if the reduction in government spending extends to ceasing export subsidies, exports will lose price competitiveness and hence, net exports will decrease, further decreasing AD. If governments implement fiscal austerity too aggressively and too suddenly, it can **therefore risk plunging the economy into a recession.**

However, if the government is able to achieve **healthier fiscal position**, and restore ability to repay debts, there will be **an increase in confidence** amongst consumers and firms. As such, **C and I may rise**, leading to an increase in AD and a multiplied increase in real GDP via the multiplier effect, thereby boosting economic growth and reducing unemployment.

Evaluation

It would be better to implement fiscal austerity bearing in mind the context and the risks of a recession. As an alternative, increasing the progressivity of incomes taxes and import tariffs can be undertaken.

A **very progressive income tax** can be undertaken. By taxing heavily on the high income earners, the government can **obtain tax revenue** while not greatly affecting consumption since the marginal propensity to consume of the high income earners is generally lower than the poor. Furthermore, the **high income earners tend to constitute a smaller percentage of the population** and therefore usually **not significant in the context of the entire economy's consumption levels**. This tax revenue can hence be used to clear government debts, simultaneously reducing income inequality.

If domestic substitutes are available, the government can consider **placing heavy tariffs on imports and use the revenue to subsidize exports**. This can help to relieve any burden on the government budget due to export subsidies. While this may invite retaliation from other countries, in the short-run, the economy may be able to obtain the stimulus it requires to recover substantially. As such, the government will be able to kick-start the economy even in a period of fiscal austerity from funds obtained via import tariffs. Alternatively, the government can **use the tariff revenues to repay debts**.

> **Tip**
>
> _Do NOT say that fiscal austerity is a form of contractionary monetary policy._ This is _WRONG_. When governments impose fiscal austerity, they do not hope that the economy will contract. In fact, often, they hope that the economy can expand in spite of the contractionary effects that austerity measures pose.

37. Explain how the Central Bank intervenes in the FOREX market.

Exchange rate (e/r) refers to the **price of a country's domestic currency in terms of foreign currency**. A country typically undertakes the macroeconomic objectives of **price stability, low unemployment, sustainable economic growth, and healthy balance of payments**. In order to achieve these macroeconomic objectives, the government may seek to appreciate or depreciate the exchange rate. This is achieved by **either buying or selling domestic currency in the foreign exchange (FOREX) market**.

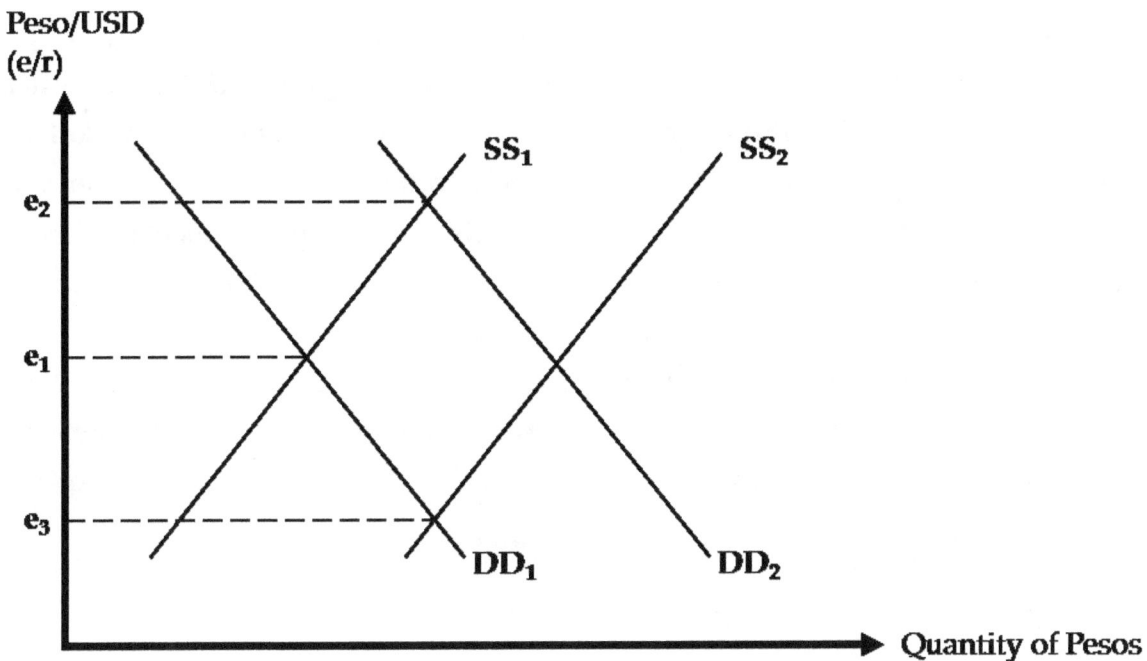

Fig 1: FOREX Market

The Mexican government may decide to appreciate the Mexican Peso's exchange rate. This is achieved by buying Mexican Peso from the FOREX market using USD from its central bank reserves. This results in an increase in demand for Mexican Peso from DD_1 to DD_2, causing the exchange rate to appreciate from e_1 to e_2. If the Mexican government wishes to pursue a depreciation, the Central Bank sells Mexican Peso in the FOREX market, causing supply to increase from SS_1 to SS_2, resulting in a depreciation from e_1 to e_3.

38. Explain how the exchange rate is determined in a managed float system.

The exchange rate (e/r) of a currency **is its price in foreign currency**. A currency's e/r **is determined by its supply and demand in the foreign exchange (FOREX) market.** Demand for a currency in the forex market is a derived demand as it is derived from foreigners' demand for the country's goods, services and assets. Supply for a country's currency is derived from the residents' demand for foreign goods, services and assets.

Singapore is an example of a country that adopts the managed-float e/r regime. Hence, the Singapore Dollar (SGD) e/r is also affected by Central Bank intervention. Firstly, the Central Bank constructs a trade weighted e/r known as the **Singapore Dollar Nominal Effective Exchange Rate (S$NEER), where the SGD is pegged against a basket of currencies of her top 10 trading partners.** Each trading partner, based on the percentage of trade Singapore engages with them, is given a "weight", which influences the degree to which the Singapore dollar e/r is pegged to the particular country. Based on this, the S$NEER is allowed to float within a band consisting of an upper limit and lower limit. This is hence known as a managed float system of e/r determination. This band is regularly revised by the Central Bank and may be gradually revised upwards. This is due to Central Bank's policy stance of a gradual and modest appreciation of the SGD.

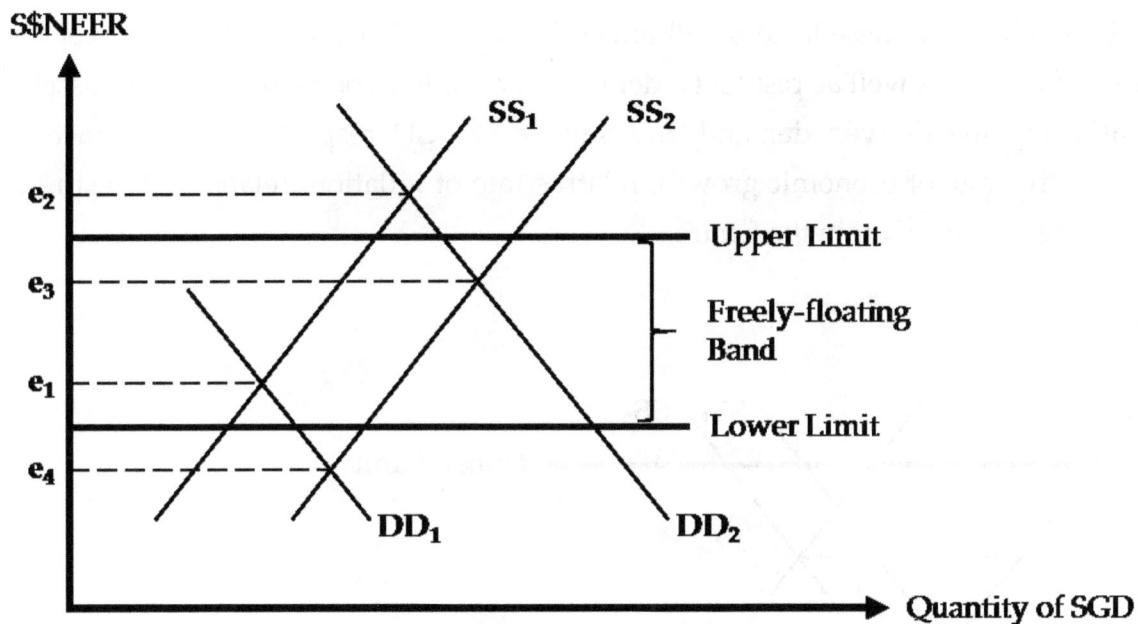

Fig 1: Managed Float Exchange Rate

Referring to Fig 1, Singapore allows her e/r to float within a range of values between the **upper** and **lower limits set by the Central Bank**. Whenever her e/r is about to breach the bands, the Central Bank will intervene in the FOREX market by either buying or selling SGD to keep the S$NEER within the bands.

For example, due to an increase in demand from DD_1 to DD_2, SGD appreciates from e_1 to e_2. As this exceeds the upper limit, the Central Bank will sell SGD in the FOREX market to increase the supply of SGD from SS_1 to SS_2, thereby depreciating the SGD from e_2 to e_3, which lies within the band.

Similarly, an increase in supply of S$ from SS_1 to SS_2 in the FOREX market causes the SGD to depreciate from e_1 to e_4, which exceeds the lower limit. The Central Bank will buy SGD in the FOREX market to increase demand from DD_1 to DD_2, thereby appreciating the SGD back from e_4 to e_3, which lies within the bands.

Within the upper and lower band, the S$NEER is allowed to float freely. This is where Singapore's e/r is determined by factors other than the Central Bank's e/r policies. These other factors that affect the e/r are also factors that will affect transactions in the Current Account (CA) and Capital and Financial Account (KFA) of the Balance of Payments

(BOP). This is because these factors will affect foreigners' demand for domestic goods, services and assets, as well as residents' demand for foreign goods, services and assets, hence affecting the derived demand and supply of SGD respectively. Such factors include relative rate of economic growth, relative rate of inflation, relative interest rate (i/r) and expectations of e/r in the future.

S$NEER

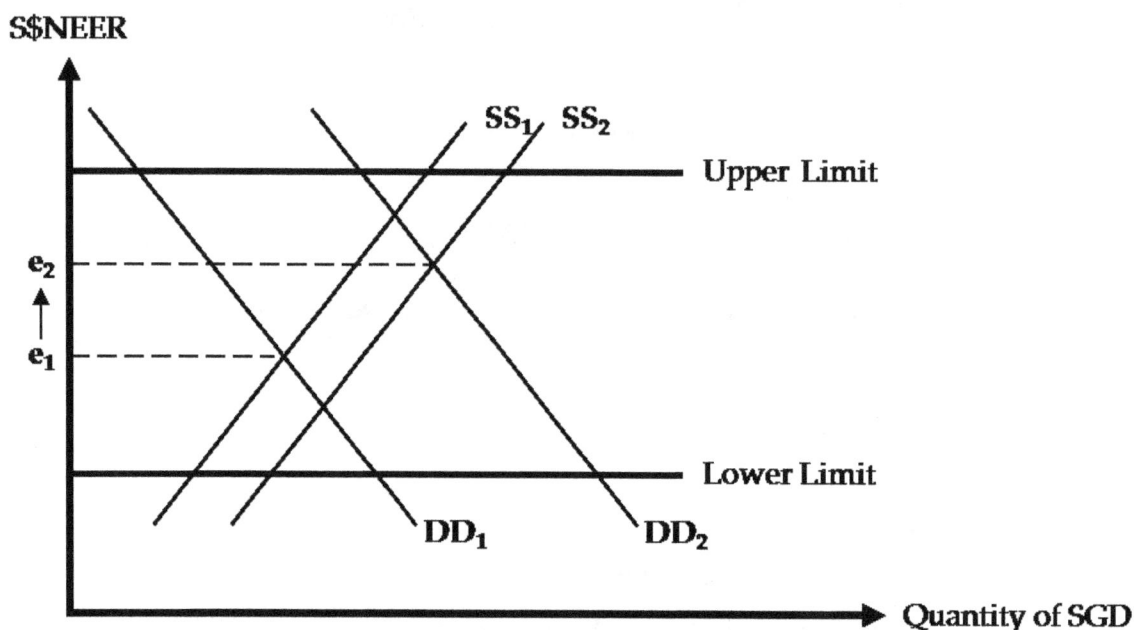

Fig 2: Appreciation Within Band

Firstly, **relative changes in incomes** can affect Singapore's e/r. Assume the incomes of both UK consumers and Singaporean consumers rise, but the incomes of UK **consumers rise faster** relative to that of Singapore's. While UK consumers' demand for Singapore's exports and Singaporean consumers' demand for UK's exports, i.e. Singapore's imports, will both increase, UK's consumption of Singapore's exports will increase by a greater extent compared to Singapore's consumption of UK's imports. As such, demand for SGD in the FOREX market will increase by a greater extent from DD_1 to DD_2 compared to supply of SGD, which will only increase from SS_1 to SS_2 in Fig 2. This results in an appreciation of SGD from e_1 to e_2.

S$NEER

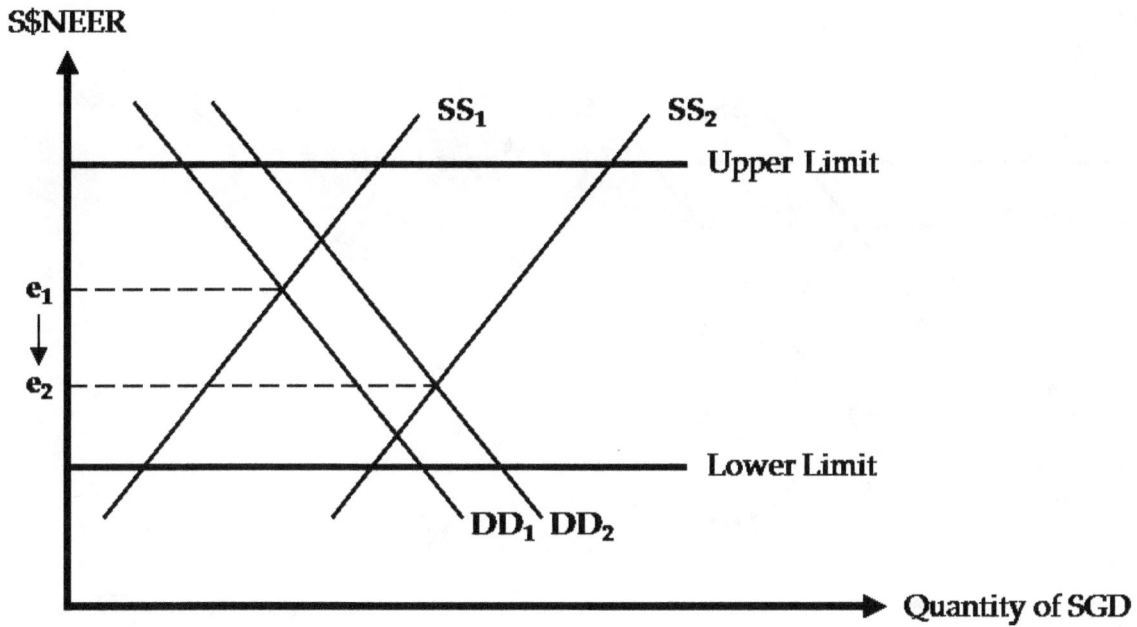

Fig 3: Depreciation Within Band

Conversely, if Singapore's income rises faster relative to that of UK, Singaporean consumers will increase their consumption of UK's imports to a greater extent that UK consumers increase their consumption of Singapore's exports. As such, supply of SGD in the FOREX market will increase by a greater extent from SS_1 to SS_2 compared to the demand for SGD, which will only increase from DD_1 to DD_2 in Fig 3. This results in a depreciation of SGD from e_1 to e_2.

S$NEER

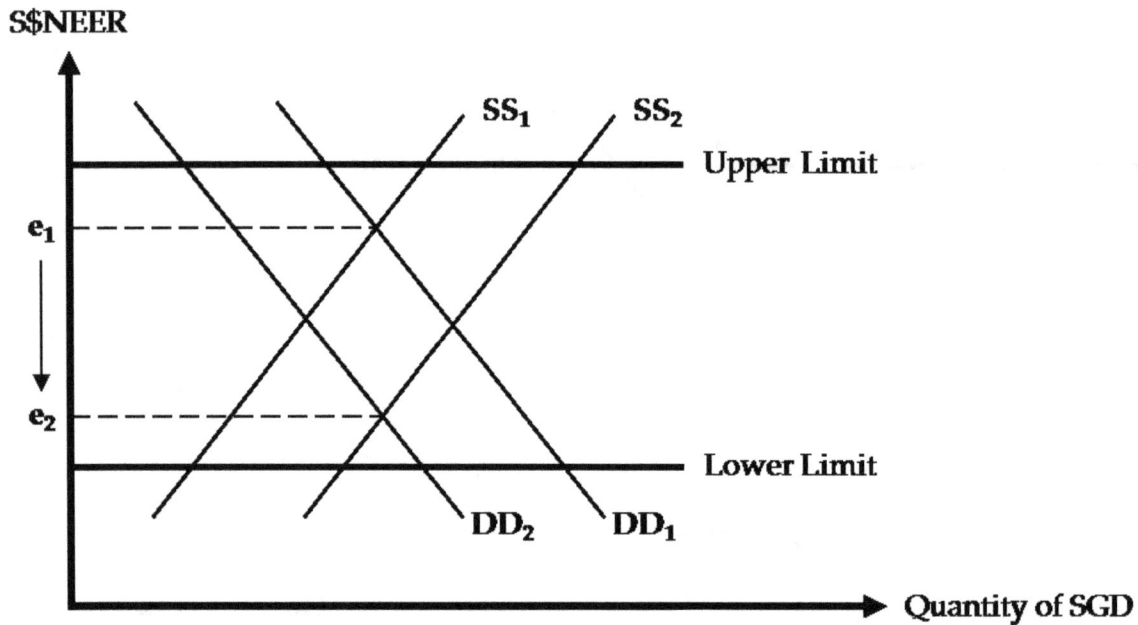

Fig 4: Depreciation Within Band

Furthermore, Singapore's inflation rate may be greater relative to the UK's, causing **British goods to become relatively cheaper**. As such, **demand** for UK's goods and exports to Singapore will increase and hence demand for the pound will increase. This will lead to an **increased supply of SGD**, from SS_1 to SS_2 in Fig 4. At the same time **UK consumers will import less from Singapore** due **to higher prices of** Singapore's exports and hence, demand for SGD will fall from DD_1 to DD_2. The **fall in demand and rise in supply** of SGD will cause depreciation from e_1 to e_2.

S$NEER

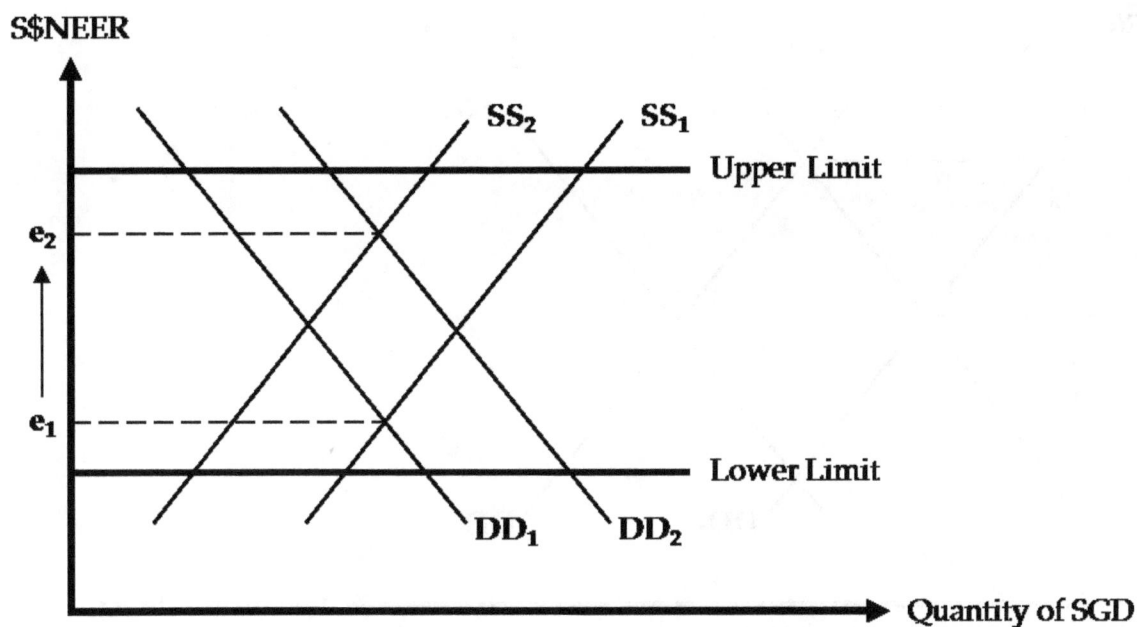

Fig 5: Appreciation Within Band

Conversely, Singapore's inflation rate may be lower relative to the UK's, causing Singapore's goods and exports to become relatively cheaper. As such, quantity demanded for Singapore's exports will rise and demand for SGD will increase from DD_1 to DD_2 in Fig 5. Concurrently, Singaporean consumers will import less from the UK as UK's goods and services have become relatively more expensive compared to locally produced goods and services. Hence, demand for UK's goods and services will fall, decreasing the demand for the pound and hence decreasing the supply of SGD from SS_1 to SS_2. The rise in demand and fall in supply of SGD will cause appreciation from e_1 to e_2.

Additionally, Singapore's i/r may be higher **relative to other countries,** which will result in **hot money inflows** which will increase the demand for SGD. This arises from **foreign investors looking to purchase short-term assets and deposit their funds into Singapore banks to earn the higher rate of interest.** Hence, **demand for SGD** increases from DD_1 to DD_2 in Fig 5. Concurrently, Singaporean investors **will cut back on investments overseas as they rather earn from the higher rate of interest domestically.** Therefore, the **supply of SGD decreases** from SS_1 to SS_2. The rise in demand and fall in supply of SGD will cause appreciation from e_1 to e_2. Conversely, referring to Fig 4 instead, a depreciation occurs when i/r in Singapore is lower relative to other countries.

S$NEER

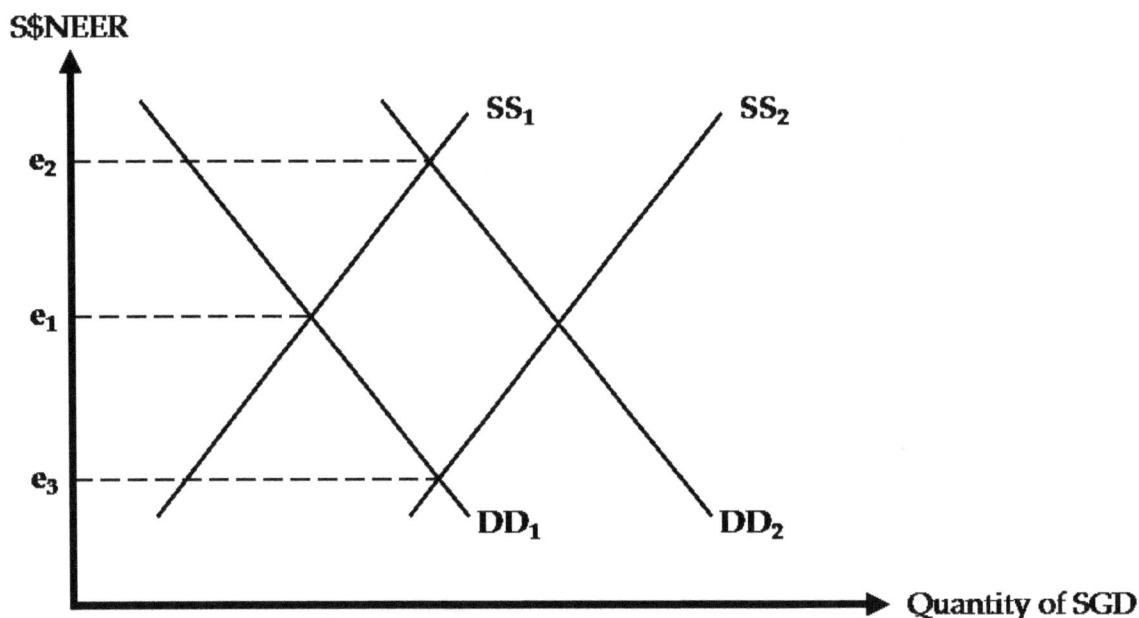

Fig 6: FOREX Market

Anticipation of e/r movements can also affect e/r. Expectations of an appreciation will lead to increased demand for SGD since investors will look to hold on to a currency that will be increasing in value. This causes a rise in demand for SGD from DD_1 to DD_2 in Fig 6, causing appreciation from e_1 to e_2. Conversely, expectations of a depreciation will lead to increased supply for SGD as investors look to offload the currency before it depreciates, resulting in an increase in supply from SS_1 to SS_2, leading to a depreciation from e_1 to e_3.

Therefore, in the case of a managed float regime like that of Singapore's, the exchange rate is determined through the interaction of demand and supply forces as well as central bank intervention.

Tip

Do NOT to say that the currency has **risen/fallen**. This is _WRONG_. It must be referred to as an *appreciation* or *depreciation* in a floating exchange rate system. In a fixed exchange-rate system, it is known as a *revaluation or devaluation*.

39. Explain how depreciating or appreciating the exchange rate can help an economy achieve its macroeconomic goals.

A depreciation in the exchange rate (e/r) can **improve the Balance of Trade (BOT)** and **attract foreign direct investments (FDI),** resulting in **greater economic growth and employment.** A depreciation is a decrease in the value of the currency in terms of foreign currency. This causes the price of exports to fall in terms of foreign currency. Assuming that demand for exports are price elastic, which is the case for most countries since there is usually significant global competition in all industries and hence a large availability of substitutes, the **quantity demanded for exports will increase more than proportionately and hence export revenue (X) will increase significantly.** Concurrently, imports become more expensive in terms of domestic currency. Assuming that the demand for imports is also price elastic, quantity demanded for imports will fall more than proportionately, thereby reducing import expenditure (M). **In fact, as long as the Marshall-Lerner Condition (MLC), which states that the sum of the price elasticities of demand for both imports and exports is greater than one i.e. $|PED_X + PED_M| > 1$, is met, the depreciation will lead to increasing net exports (X-M) and improve BOT.** Since BOT is the main component of the Current Account (CA), the CA is likely to improve, helping to achieve a healthy Balance of Payments (BOP).

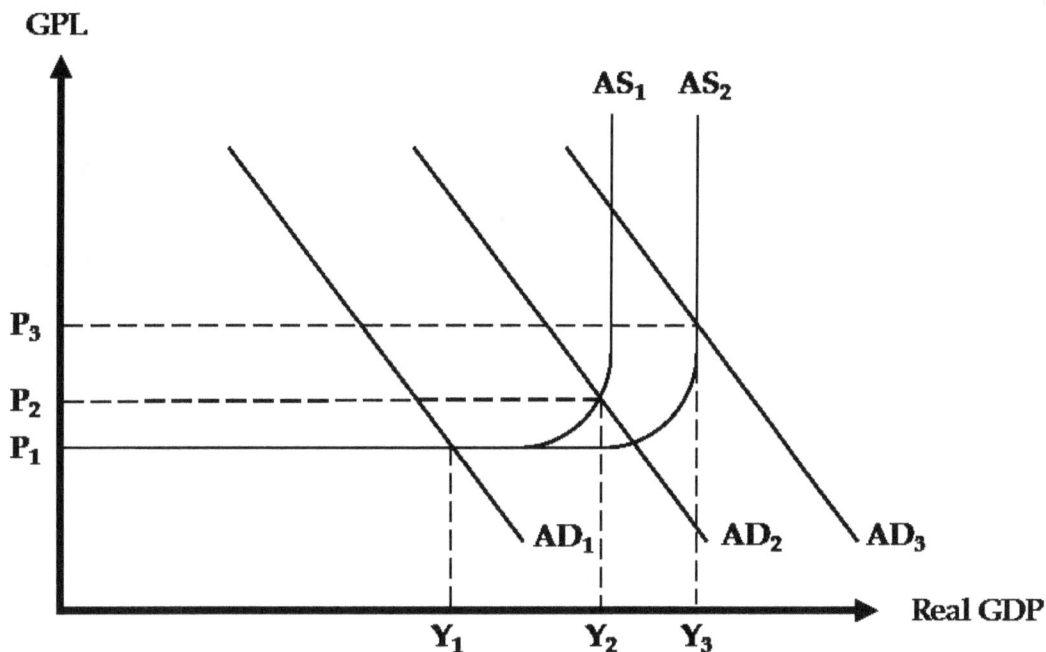

Fig 1: Depreciation and Economic Growth

The **increase in X-M results in an increase in aggregate demand (AD) from AD_1 to AD_2 in Fig 1**, which will result in a shortfall in stocks and inventories of firms, thereby prompting firms to increase output. Real GDP will increase by a multiplied amount of the initial increase in X-M, from Y_1 to Y_2 via the multiplier process, hence achieving actual economic growth. The increase in production will cause firms to increase derived demand for factors of production such as labour, reducing unemployment.

A depreciation also **causes the initial cost of investment by foreign firms to decrease**. This may increase the expected rate of return of investing in the country and hence, increase the influx of FDIs, thereby improving the Capital and Financial Account (KFA) balance, helping to achieve a healthy BOP. Furthermore, as the influx of FDI is likely to involve increased spending on capital goods in the economy, such as new factories, equipment and machinery. Investments (I) will increase leading to an increase in AD from AD_2 to AD_3. The FDI influx will also increase the amount of available capital goods and greater levels of technology, leading to potential growth as long-run aggregate supply (LRAS) increases and shifts aggregate supply (AS) curve from AS_1 to AS_2. The rise in both AD and LRAS results in an increase in real GDP from Y_2 to Y_3. Hence, it is evident that a depreciation can improve the BOT, BOP since both CA and KFA balances improve, drive actual and potential economic growth and increase employment.

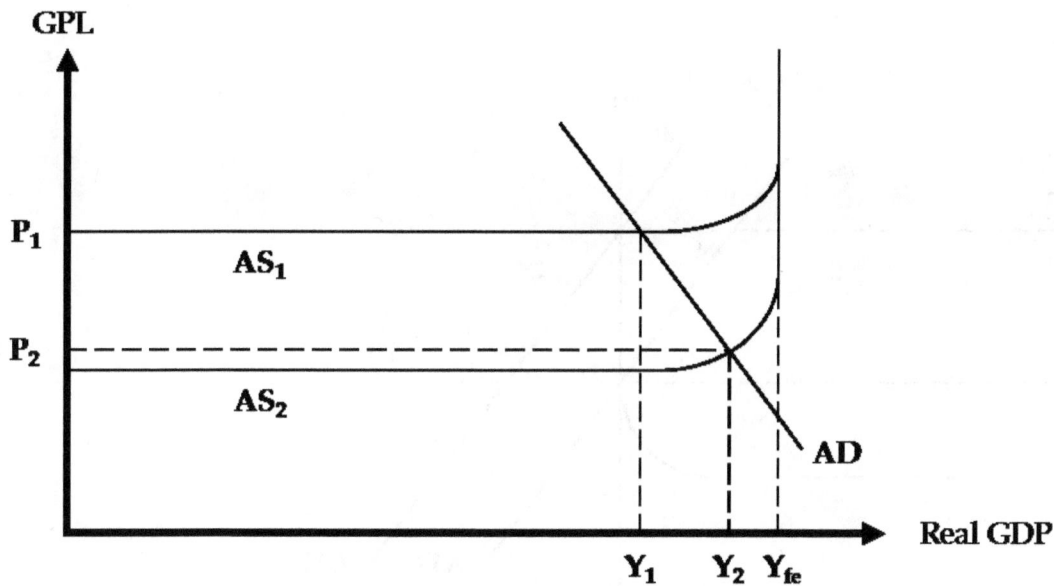

Fig 2: Appreciation and Lower Cost-Push Inflation

An appreciation in the exchange rate can **help to reduce imported cost-push inflation.** Because of an appreciation, both imports of raw materials and final goods and services become cheaper in terms of domestic currency. This reduces the unit cost of production and increases the short-run AS (SRAS) of the economy, shifting AS curve downwards from AS_1 to AS_2. Firms are willing and able to produce more output at each and every price level, and the excess supply will lead to a fall in prices, thereby resulting in a fall in general price levels (GPL) from P_1 to P_2. Hence, imported cost-push inflation is curbed.

GPL

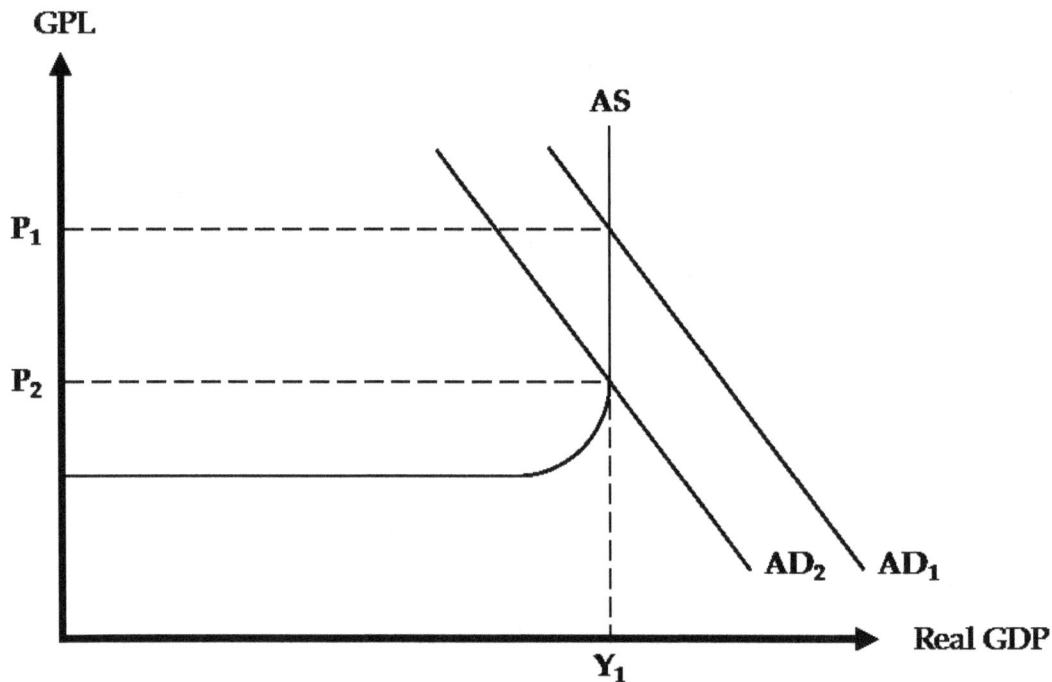

Fig 3: Appreciation and Reduced Demand-pull Inflation

Furthermore, an appreciation can **reduce demand-pull inflation.** As the price of exports in terms of foreign currency increases, quantity demanded for exports will increase, resulting in a fall in X. Concurrently, imports become cheaper in terms of domestic currency and quantity demanded for imports therefore increases, resulting in a rise in M. Due to a fall in X and rise in M, X-M will fall, leading to a fall in AD from AD_1 to AD_2 in Fig 3. The reduced level of production and hence reduced competition for scarce factors of production will result in a decrease in GPL from P_1 to P_2, thereby curbing demand-pull inflation.

Evaluation

Especially Effective for Small and Open Economies

The e/r policy is **especially effective for small and open economies (SOEs), who** have **a limited domestic market and are extremely trade dependent.** As such, SOEs **rely on external demand and X to drive economic growth.** Because of the **lack of natural resources, they are also very import dependent.** For example, for large economies like USA, X takes up just 15-20% of USA's GDP, while for SOEs like Singapore, X amounts to about 200% of Singapore's GDP, thereby reflecting the enormous dependence on exports. Hence, because X takes up a much larger proportion of GDP than any other component of AD, exchange rate policy is especially powerful for SOEs since **e/r is able to directly influence X-M and hence AD**, driving economic growth, reducing unemployment, ensuring healthy BOP and low inflation rates. E/r policies can also help to curb imported inflation, which is a key source of inflation for SOEs given their heavy dependence on imported raw materials.

> Key Statistics to show dependence on exports Singapore: X/GDP = 200%, C/GDP = 40%   US: X/GDP = 15-20%, C/GDP = 70%

E/r policy is also **more effective than interest rate (i/r) policy since SOEs are usually highly open to capital flows and are i/r takers.** SOEs are **too small to influence world i/r.** In addition, their **openness to trade, services and capital flows causes them to be unable to control money supply, and are hence unable to independently set their own i/r.** This is due to the fact that **if the Central Bank increases i/r,** foreign investors will look to invest there seeking higher rates of return. **Hence, there will be hot money inflows**, made possible due to free capital flows. This will **increase the amount of loanable funds** in banks, **thereby reducing i/r and rendering the i/r policy ineffective.** Hence, i/r policy is not feasible in SOEs, further emphasizing the need for e/r policy.

Less Effective for Large Economies

However, just as e/r policy is especially effective for SOEs, large economies that are less dependent on external demand and imports will find e/r policy to be less effective. **USA, a large economy, has 60-70% of GDP comprising of domestic consumption while Singapore, a SOE, only has 40%.** As such, any cyclical unemployment faced by large economies is likely to be caused by low domestic consumption. In such a case, expansionary fiscal and monetary i/r policies will be more effective in driving economic growth and reducing unemployment. Conversely, in the event of demand-pull inflation, contractionary fiscal and monetary i/r policies would also be more effective in cooling down domestic demand to reduce demand-pull inflation.

Conflicts in Macroeconomic Goals

The e/r policy **cannot achieve all the macro goals at the same time**. For example, depreciation of currency to increase export competitiveness to spur economic growth may lead to higher imported inflation. Hence, the government has to choose the most pertinent problems to target and decide on whether to pursue appreciation or depreciation at any point in time. Other macro goals may also need to be achieved via other policies.

Necessity of Foreign Exchange Reserves

The e/r policy requires the Central Bank to have **sufficient amounts of foreign exchange reserves** in order to effectively appreciate the currency. Over time, a persistent need to appreciate the e/r or hold up a naturally depreciating exchange rate may wear down the foreign exchange reserves of the Central Bank. Upon depletion, e/r policy can no longer be utilised. Moreover, when foreign reserves are depleted, the country's currency is also likely to face speculative currency attacks, thereby causing the e/r to depreciate very quickly. An example would be the Thai Baht and Indonesian Rupiah during the 1991 Asian Financial Crisis. As such, it is not effective for countries that do not possess large amounts of foreign exchange reserves or persistently face a BOP deficit to pursue e/r interventions.

May Not Improve BOT

A **depreciation may not necessarily improve the BOT**. Firstly, MLC may not hold. This is because in the short-run, the demand for exports and imports may be price-inelastic due to contractual obligations and time required to search for other substitutes. As such, $|PED_x + PED_M|$ may not necessarily be more than 1. In such a case, a depreciation may cause the converse of the intended effect, resulting in X-M falling instead of rising. See Chapter 28 for a detailed explanation on the J-Curve Effect.

Secondly, there may be a **reduction in FDI inflows, as profits earned when converted and repatriated back to home country will now be reduced due to the depreciation. Hence foreign firms may now** expect a lowered rate of return on investment and may be deterred from investing. Furthermore, depreciation can also cause an increase in hot money outflows and a fall in hot money inflows as investors look to invest in appreciating currencies. These will cause a deterioration to the KFA as well as the BOP.

Does Not Tackle Root Cause

The e/r policy is **not effective when the root cause of the economic problems are supply-side related**. A lack of potential growth hindering actual growth cannot be significantly addressed by e/r policy. Similarly, structural unemployment and wage-push inflation are supply-side problems that cannot be rectified by adjusting e/r. For such problems, supply-side policies such as providing incentives to increase investments in capital equipment, human resource, as well as aligning wage growth with productivity growth are needed to ensure an increase in potential growth and a fall in the unit costs of production.

40. Explain the usefulness of short-run supply-side policies.

Short-run supply-side policies aim to lower the unit cost of production and increase the short-run aggregate supply (SRAS). This can result in **actual growth, decrease unemployment, alleviate inflation**, and help achieve **healthy Balance of Payments (BOP)**.

The SRAS is affected largely by unit costs of production and hence **prices of factor inputs.** Supply-side policies are aimed at **lowering unit costs of production (COP).** For example, this can be achieved through wage policies and subsidies. During the 2009 US Financial crisis, the Singapore government implemented a wage subsidy in the form of the **Jobs Credits Scheme**. This scheme subsidizes labour costs by paying for part of workers' wages, therefore lowering the unit labour cost and hence the unit COP and increasing the SRAS. Another example is the Indian government implementing subsidies such as on fuel, which is a factor of production involved in most industries hence lowering unit COP and increasing SRAS. Market-oriented supply-side policies can also be implemented. Lowering or even removing the minimum wage will lower unit labour cost and unit COP because the minimum wage is set above the equilibrium wage, increasing SRAS. Deregulation, liberalisation and pro-competition policies all aim to increase level of competition between firms, resulting in greater productive efficiency as complacency is reduced and cost-cutting measures by firms are introduced to lower unit COP and hence increase SRAS.

GPL

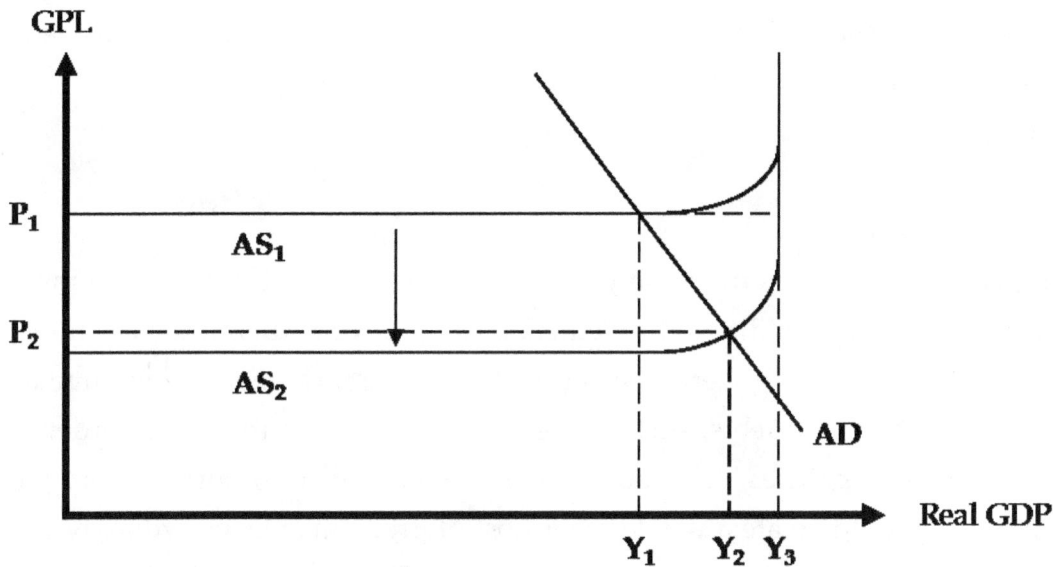

Fig 1: Short-run Supply-side Policies

The **increase in SRAS** is represented as a downward shift of the SRAS from AS_1 to AS_2 in Fig 1. This means that firms are now willing and able to produce more at each and every general price level (GPL). Hence, at the prevailing GPL of P_1, actual output temporarily increases to Y_3 while quantity demanded remains at Y_1. This results in a **surplus of Y_1Y_3**. Due to this surplus, firms will reduce output and also cut prices to clear stocks as there is unplanned increase in stocks and inventories. As firms reduce output, competition for resources decreases, contributing to the **fall in GPL** from P_1 to P_2. As the GPL falls to P_2, **quantity demanded increases** from Y_1 to Y_2 due to the wealth, interest rate and international substitution effects (movement along AD). At Y_2, where the AD intersects AS_2, the **surplus is eliminated** and the economy has reached a **new equilibrium**. Real GDP has increased from Y_1 to Y_2, representing actual growth. As firms increase production they will also hire more workers and this leads to a fall in unemployment. Furthermore, there has been a fall in GPL, alleviating any existing inflationary pressures in the economy.

The fall in GPL will also mean that exports are now cheaper and more price-competitive, and hence assuming that the demand for exports are price elastic, export revenue (X) will increase. Concurrently import expenditure (M) will fall since domestic alternatives have become cheaper and households therefore reduce their demand for import. The increasing net exports (X-M) would help improve the balance of trade (BOT) and in turn help improve the BOP.

Evaluation

Short-run supply-side policies in the form of subsidies require significant government spending and a government's ability to implement such policies is therefore very much dependent on the health of the government budget. Furthermore, many governments today are in huge government debts, such as the EU countries and the US. In order to finance these supply-side policies, such governments would have to borrow from the private sector, which would create a whole other host of problems like crowding out of investments. This budget could be better spent in areas of healthcare and education to increase the productive capacity of the economy and improve the non-material welfare of the people. Hence, the benefits of implementing such policies must be properly weighed against its opportunity costs.

Given the long gestation period of long-run supply-side policies, in dire situations, short-run supply side policies can provide a necessary short term solution to boost growth, reduce unemployment and lower the rate of inflation.

41. Explain the effect of an increase in labour productivity on the economy.

Labour productivity is defined as the **amount of output produced per worker hour.** It tends to be affected by **the quality of labour, amount of capital goods, and level of technology.** Increasing labour productivity will help to **drive down unit labour costs,** thereby reducing unit costs of production (COP) assuming the extent of increase in labour productivity exceeds the extent of increases in wages.

Unit labour cost measures the **cost of labour per unit of output**. If wages increase more than labour productivity, unit labour cost will increase. Conversely, if the growth in labour productivity exceeds the increase in wages, unit labour cost falls. The fall in unit labour costs thereby leads to a fall in unit COP, increasing the short-run aggregate supply (SRAS), resulting in actual growth, lower unemployment, reduced rate of inflation and improvement in the Balance of Payments (BOP). Furthermore, increasing labour productivity can also expand the productive capacity of an economy and increase long-run aggregate supply (LRAS), hence contributing to potential growth.

Besides through increasing the quality of labour, the increase in labour productivity can also come about through acquiring more capital goods, and technological advancements. Therefore, the pursuit of increasing labour productivity would also result in an **expansion of the economy's productive capacity**. Part of skills training and education includes equipping workers with skills to operate and utilize large, sophisticated capital goods in production. As labour productivity increases through workers obtaining skills and knowledge to operate such capital goods, the production process and technology employed becomes more advanced. Existing resources can be made use of more efficiently to result in greater levels of output than before. The increase in quality of labour and technological advancements that increase productive capacity will increase LRAS, ensuring potential growth which is essential for sustainable, non-inflationary economic growth.

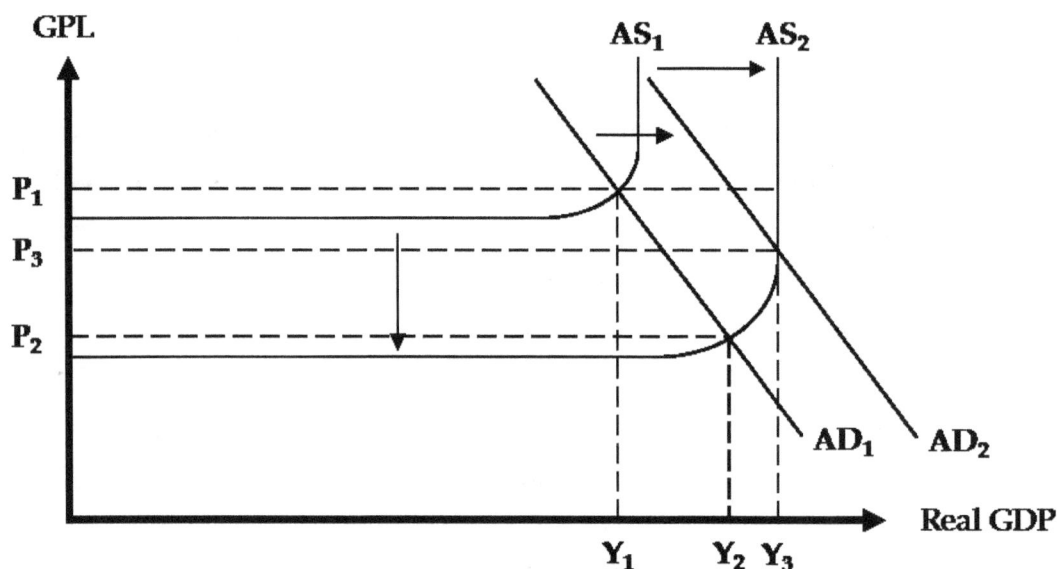

Fig 1: Increasing Labour Productivity

The increase in both SRAS and LRAS is represented by an outward shift in the AS curve from AS_1 to AS_2 in Fig 1. This means that firms are now willing and able to produce more at each and every GPL. Hence, at the prevailing GPL of P_1, actual output temporarily increases to Y_3 while quantity demanded remains at Y_1, resulting in a **surplus of Y_1Y_3**. Due to this surplus, firms will reduce output and also cut prices to clear stocks as there is unplanned increase in stocks and inventories. As firms reduce output, competition for resources decreases, contributing to the **fall in GPL** from P_1 to P_2. As GPL falls to P_2, **quantity demanded increases** from Y_1 to Y_2 due to the wealth, interest rate and international effects. Assuming that aggregate demand (AD) is originally at AD_1, at Y_2, where AD_1 intersects AS_2, the **surplus is eliminated** and the economy has reached a **new equilibrium**. Real GDP has increased from Y_1 to Y_2, hence actual growth. As firms increase production they also hire more workers, leading to a fall in unemployment. Furthermore, there has been a fall in GPL, alleviating cost-push inflationary pressures in the economy. The increase in productive capacity and LRAS, on the other hand, alleviates future demand-pull inflationary pressures.

The fall in GPL will also mean that exports are now cheaper, and hence assuming that the demand for exports are price elastic, export revenue (X) will increase. With better quality workers, higher quality (e.g. more durable and reliable) goods and services may be produced, thus increasing non-price competitiveness of exports, increasing demand for exports and hence increasing X. Concurrently import expenditure (M) will fall since domestic alternatives have become cheaper and households therefore reduce their demand for imports. These would help improve the Balance of Trade (BOT), and improve the Current Account (CA) balance. Moreover, the lower unit COP will increase the expected rate of return on investments. This will attract more FDI inflows and improve the Capital and Financial Account (KFA) balance. Since the CA and KFA balances improve, the overall BOP will improve.

The increase in FDI will usually lead to an increase in investments (I). This, together with increased X, results in an increase in AD from AD_1 to AD_2, increasing real GDP by a multiplied amount via the multiplier effect, resulting in further actual economic growth.

Evaluation

The likelihood of an increase in labour productivity exceeding the extent of wage increase is very much dependent on the **strength of labour unions** in the country and the existing labour legislations. The stronger the unions and the more pro-worker the legislations, increases in labour productivity may not lead to a significant fall in unit COP.

Deliberate government policies have to be implemented to increase labour productivity. They suffer from some of the same problems that long-run supply-side policies face. Foremost, it may take a long time for workers to be trained and educated. Therefore an economic slowdown may persist as productivity and competitiveness will not increase anytime soon. Furthermore, the effectiveness of training depends on the workers' mindsets. If workers are not receptive towards picking up new skills and changing methods of production, productivity will not increase. Such policies also tend to strain the government's budget. Opportunity cost incurred may include better healthcare and education facilities. These opportunity costs have to be weighed against how likely policies will succeed in raising the labour productivity and the benefits of doing so.

42. Explain market-oriented supply-side policies.

Market-oriented supply-side policies are targeted at enabling free markets to function more efficiently by encouraging competition and improving market incentives. In doing so, unit costs of production (COP) can be lowered and productive capacity expanded, resulting in an increase in both short-run (SRAS) and long-run aggregate supply (LRAS).

Pro-competition policies **increase competitiveness in the market** by providing the **impetus for innovation and more efficient ways of production**. Usually, these come in the form of deregulation and liberalization of market so as to reduce barriers to entry as well as laws that prohibit abuse of market power, the formation of monopolies (e.g. governing over mergers and acquisitions of dominant firms) and collusion between oligopolies. By increasing competition, firms are forced to cut inefficiencies and to innovate to find more cost-efficient methods of production. As such, it prevents SRAS from falling as unit COP is kept low. For example, in many cities, utilities are provided by monopolies. This can result in high costs for firms. By increasing the contestability in the utilities industry, the cost of utilities will fall, thereby decreasing COP across all industries, increasing the **SRAS**. As firms continue to innovate on production methods and create new technologies, **the LRAS can also increase**. The reduced inefficiencies will also free up scarce resources which can be channelled to produce more goods and services, thus also enabling an increase in the LRAS.

Furthermore, the government can also reform labour laws to allow the labour market to work efficiently. For example, the government may remove minimum wage laws or pass laws to curtail the power of trade unions. These tend to reduce wages and therefore unit COP in the economy, **increasing the SRAS**.

Governments can also **cut taxes to ensure competitive corporate tax rates**. This will increase the level of investments as the expected rate of return from investment projects increases. As investments increase, **more capital goods** are added to the economy hence **increasing the productive capacity of the economy and thus increasing the LRAS.**

The government can also **decrease personal income taxes and reduce unemployment benefits (unemployment benefits increase the opportunity cost of working)** to increase the incentive to work. This can increase the **quantity of the workforce** and hence **the productive capacity of the economy and thus increasing the LRAS**.

GPL

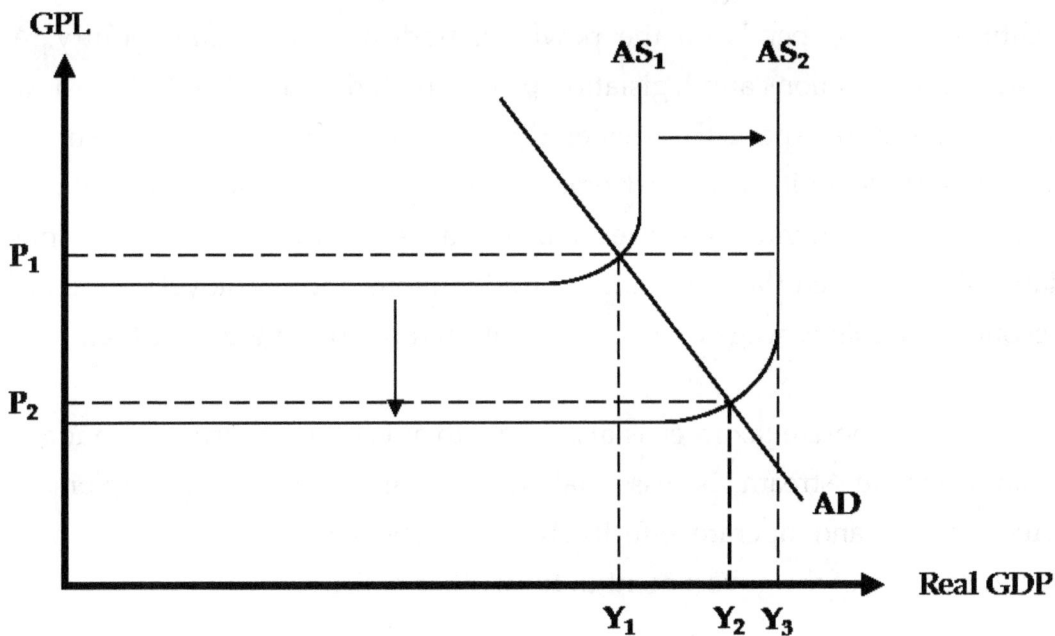

Fig 1: Market-oriented Supply-side Policies

The combined increase in both SRAS and LRAS due to market-oriented supply-side policies is represented by an outward shift in the AS from AS_1 to AS_2 in Fig 1. This means that firms are now willing and able to produce more at each and every GPL. Hence, real GDP has increased from Y_1 to Y_2, hence there is actual growth. As firms increase production they will also hire more workers and this leads to a fall in unemployment. Furthermore, there has been a fall in GPL, curbing cost-push inflation. The increase in productive capacity and LRAS means that the economy is able to produce greater amount of output at full employment, hence there is potential growth. This can also alleviate future demand-pull inflationary pressures.

Hence, market-oriented supply-side policies have resulted in a fall in GPL and an increase in real output. It is therefore instrumental in allowing for sustainable, non-inflationary economic growth.

Evaluation

However, there will usually be huge political resistance against abolishing minimum wage laws. Ultimately, it depends on the power of trade unions in the country. A country with strong trade unions and legislation protecting individuals' right to protest and expression is likely to experience greater difficulty in managing wages. This is especially so when trade unions are extremely uncompromising or belligerent. In contrast, the Singapore government has established a very strong and harmonious tripartite relationship between the government, trade unions and employers. This has allowed the economy to follow wage freeze guidelines in times of severe recession.

Furthermore, a cut in corporate tax rates is also likely to affect the government budget. A constant tax revenue stream is essential for the government to implement macroeconomic policies and operate effectively. Lowering corporate tax rates may therefore affect the ability of the government to fulfil other policies.

It is also not easy for the government to effectively check against collusive behaviour and abuse of market power, as firms would have every incentive to hide such behaviours. It can also be a strain on government resources to investigate and follow through legal processes in order to enforce the competition laws.

43. Explain the usefulness of long-run supply-side policies.

Long-run supply-side policies refer to policies that are aimed at increasing the quality or quantity of resources in the economy to expand its productive capacity. This is seen from Fig 1 below where the vertical section of the AS, which represents long-run aggregate supply (LRAS), shifts rightwards and the full employment level of output increases from Y_1 to Y_3. Thus, long-run supply-side policies result in potential growth and aid in achieving **sustainable, non-inflationary growth, which is growth where increase in aggregate demand (AD) is accompanied by a corresponding increase in aggregate supply (AS)**, allowing an increase in real GDP with reduced demand-pull inflation.

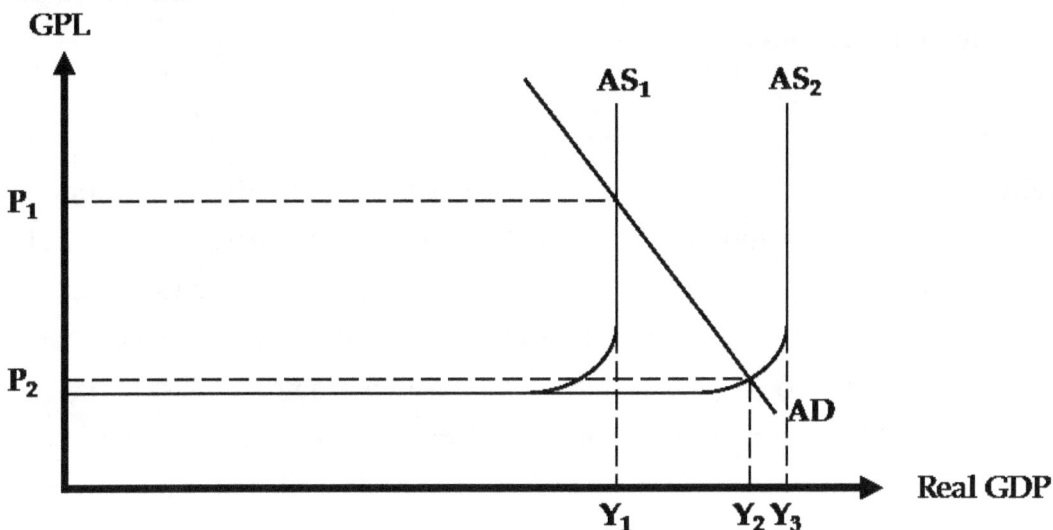

Fig 1: Long-run Supply-side Policies

Long-run supply-side policies increase the quality and quantity of factors of production, such as land, labour, capital goods and entrepreneurship in the economy, allowing it to produce more output. As the **quantity** or **quality of resources** have increased, resources are **less scarce than before** and hence, **firms compete less with one another** for factors of production, resulting in a **fall in prices of inputs** and hence, a **fall in the general price level (GPL)** from P_1 to P_2. Furthermore, the **greater spare capacity** in the economy allows it to produce at greater levels than before, resulting an increase in real GDP from Y_1 to Y_2.

The government can undertake **population policies** like encouraging higher birth rates or attracting migrants. For example, Singapore actively attracts foreign talents for the biomedical and IT sectors. Furthermore, she constantly tries to increase birth rates by giving incentives for having children such as the Baby Bonus Scheme which awards tax relief and monetary support for every additional child. The influx of foreign workers, foreign talents and increased birth rate will increase both quantity and quality of labour, increasing the productive capacity of the economy.

Furthermore, **technological advancements** provide more efficient methods of production that yield greater output from fewer inputs. The government can fund **research and development** projects to research new methods of production including through developing more technologically advanced capital goods. This will increase the productive capacity of the economy.

Additionally, **investing in infrastructure** like roads, airports, railways, and communication networks increases levels of efficiency and productivity. With modern, efficient infrastructure, scarce resources can be better utilised to increase output levels. For example, Singapore invests in an intricately connected network of roads. She also boasts one of the most well-connected broadband services in the world. These enable her workers to commute and communicate with ease, thereby increasing labour productivity. This has allowed Singapore to alleviate her problem of the lack of natural resources and small workforce. By increasing the amount and quality of infrastructure, all her other factors of production are able to be utilised with greater efficiency, resulting in greater output with the same scarce resources.

Evaluation

However, supply-side policies are limited by their highly uncertain outcomes. Measures taken by the government to increase birth-rate may not necessarily work, and in Singapore, they have been largely ineffective. Augmenting the domestic workforce with foreigners can also lead to a whole host of other problems such as social tensions which will eventually lead to political and economic instability.

In addition, the positive effects will take a long time to come to fruition. In certain instances, macroeconomic problems may be very pressing, requiring urgent solutions. For example, a country may be experiencing massive Balance of Payments (BOP) deficits stemming from a loss in economic competitiveness. While supply-side policies will be able to tackle the root of this problem for example by retraining and educating the workforce, as well as building appropriate infrastructure, such policies will take a few years to come to fruition. In such instances, other policies such as short-run supply-side policies and even protectionism may be required to prevent a BOP crisis.

Most long-run supply-side policies can be extremely straining on the government budget. It can only be afforded by governments with healthy budget surpluses and significant government reserves. Many governments in developed economies today are facing huge budget deficits and public debts. Therefore, long-run supply-side policies may not always be feasible.

44. Explain the theory of comparative advantage.

Comparative advantage refers to the **ability to produce a good or product at a lower opportunity cost**. According to the theory of comparative advantage, a country should **specialize in the production of goods that it has comparative advantage in** and **export them**, and **import goods in which it does not have comparative advantage in**.

Comparative advantage arises because of **different factor endowments** in different countries. Some countries have relative abundant of land and labour, as well as suitable weather and hence enjoy comparative advantage in producing agricultural products like rice while some countries have relatively greater abundance of highly skilled and knowledgeable workforce as well as advanced technology which gives it comparative advantage in producing high-value-added goods like computer software. Assuming in both Singapore and Thailand, 50% of each country's resources are allocated to rice production while the remaining 50% are allocated to computer production.

Production Before Specialization Showing Opportunity Cost Ratios

	Rice	Computers	Opportunity cost of producing 1 unit of rice	Opportunity cost of producing 1 unit of computer
Singapore	50	200	200/50 = 4 computers	50/200 = 0.25 rice
Thailand	200	50	50/200 = 0.25 computer	200/50 = 4 rice
Total World Output	250	250		

For the same amount of resources distributed evenly between the production of rice and computers, Singapore can produce 50 units of rice and 200 units of computers. Thailand can produce 200 units of rice and 50 units of computers. Hence, to produce one unit of computers, Thailand has to forgo 4 units of rice production. To produce 1 unit of computer, Singapore only has to forgo 0.25 units of rice production. Hence, Singapore has comparative advantage in the production of computers as it incurs lower opportunity cost than Thailand. Similarly, to produce 1 unit of rice, Singapore has to forgo 4 units of computers, while Thailand only has to forgo 0.25 units of computers.

Hence, Thailand has comparative advantage in the production of rice since it incurs a lower opportunity cost in its production.

Production After Specialization

	Rice	Computers	Opportunity cost of producing 1 unit of rice	Opportunity cost of producing 1 unit of computer
Singapore	0	400	200/50 = 4 computers	50/200 = 0.25 rice
Thailand	400	0	50/200 = 0.25 computer	200/50 = 4 rice
Total World Output	400	400		

After complete specialization, Singapore will produce 400 units of computers while Thailand will produce 400 units of rice. As such, total world output for computers and rice will have increased from 250 units to 400 units respectively. World Output would therefore have increased by 400 – 250 = 150 units of rice and 150 units of computers.

Terms of Trade

Terms of trade refer to the **rate at which one product can be exchanged for another product**. For this example, it is the rate for which rice can be exchange for computers, and vice versa. Singapore's **opportunity cost ratio is 1 rice : 4 computers**. This means that Singapore **will not pay more than 4 computers for every unit of rice** because then Singapore would be better off producing rice herself. Similarly, Thailand's opportunity cost ratio is 1 computer : 4 rice, and **will not accept less than 0.25 unit of computer for each unit of rice.**

Hence, the terms of trade of rice will be 0.25 computer < 1 rice < 4 computers.

Gains From Trade

Assume that the terms of trade is 1 unit of computer for 1 unit of rice. Hence, consumption levels will be as follows:

	Rice	Computers	Gains from trade (rice)	Gains from trade (computers)
Singapore	100	300	100 – 50 = 50	300 – 200 = 100
Thailand	300	100	300 – 200 = 100	100 – 50 = 50
Total World Consumption	400	400		

With trade, Singapore will be able to consume 100 units of rice and 300 units of computers, while Thailand will be able to consume 300 units of rice and 100 units of computers. Singapore therefore benefits from trade, gaining an extra 50 units of rice and 100 units of computers. Thailand gains an extra 100 units of rice and 50 units of computers. Both countries are **hence able to consume at higher levels than before**, resulting in higher standards of living. As the world output has also increased, specialization via comparative advantage represents an **efficient global allocation of resources**.

Evaluation

It must be noted that trade does not always take place in accordance to the theory of comparative advantage. For example, Singapore may still choose to produce rice instead of relying on imports from Thailand, due to strategic reasons. Should there be a political conflict in future, Thailand may decide to stop exporting rice to Singapore, and this would harm her survival since food is a necessity and rice is a staple. Hence despite the gains that can be reaped from specialisation and trade, it may not happen or may not happen to the fullest extent.

45. What are the determinants of a country's pattern of trade?

Pattern of trade refers to the **composition and direction of a country's exports and imports** as well as that of her trading partners. There are **2 distinctive patterns of trade**: **inter-industry trade** and **intra-industry trade.** Inter-industry trade depends on a **country's factor endowments while intra-industry trade is motivated by consumers' differing tastes and preferences.** Government trade policies can affect both inter-industry and intra-industry trade.

<u>Inter-Industry Trade and Relative Factor Endowments</u>

Inter-industry trade refers to trade that occurs between countries across completely different sectors of goods and services. This is largely based upon the theory of comparative advantage (CA), which states that countries stand to gain from trade if they specialise and exchange goods and services based on differences in opportunity costs. Countries **export products that they have a comparative advantage in (lower opportunity cost in producing) while importing products that they have a higher opportunity cost in producing.**

For example, Singapore's pattern of trade can be explained via her factor endowments. Her factor endowments include a **well-educated and trained labour force**, good **infrastructure,** and **advanced technology.** These are all very suitable for **knowledge-intensive, technology-intensive,** high-value **products.** On the other hand, Singapore **severely lacks cheap labour and natural resources such as mineral deposits and land for agricultural activities and labour-intensive manufacturing.** Hence, in order to exploit gains from specialization according to the theory of comparative advantage, Singapore imports products that she has a higher opportunity cost in producing like agriculture and primary commodities like metals and low-end manufactured wares.

Hence, Singapore's exports include **high value-added products** that are capital and knowledge-intensive, such as electronics, bio-medicals, petrochemicals, marine oil rigs and ship repair services. Examples of high-value added services that are exported include water management, hospital management, and airport and seaport management. On the other hand, Singapore imports agricultural products as well as labour-intensive goods and services like textiles and lower value added consumer electronics from economies such as China and Vietnam.

Intra-Industry Trade

Intra-industry trade refers to trade that occurs between countries that **possess similar comparative advantage.** While this contradicts the theory of comparative advantage, it can be explained by consumers' tastes and preferences and globalization. Consumers have differing tastes and preferences, and will hence **demand variety in goods and services**. For example, even if Singapore manufactures Creative MP3 players, consumers may not be satisfied with just one brand of MP3 players, and may demand other foreign brands like Japan's Sony and USA's Apple. Hence, Singapore can trade Creative MP3 players for Sony and Apple MP3 players in order to provide greater variety for Singaporean consumers. Hence, **intra-industry trade results in greater consumer satisfaction.**

Globalisation

Furthermore, the advent of Globalization has also affected the pattern of trade. With globalization, **more economies have opened up to trade**. This intensifies the competition across economies and can result in **rapidly shifting CA** and changing patterns of trade. For example, the United States has lost comparative advantage in automobile manufacturing and textiles to economies like Vietnam and China, which has opened up to trade in the last couple of decades. This has resulted in a decline in the exports of such goods and services for the US, while instead importing more from the countries with comparative advantage.

About 30 years ago, Singapore possessed comparative advantage in the manufacturing of textiles. That comparative advantage has since been lost to China. Hence, globalization has also shifted Singapore's pattern of trade significantly. However, taking advantage of globalisation, Singapore continually attempts to attract more FDI and foreign talents to **develop new areas of comparative advantage** in industries such as the Biomedical. Hence **globalisation provides the opportunity to alter factor**

endowments and Singapore has successfully built up the Biomedical industry as a key export sector.

Government Policies

Government policies for example to enact **protectionism or to pursue Free trade Agreements** will have significant impact on the pattern of trade. Free trade agreements are legally binding agreements between 2 or more countries to reduce trade barriers and promote freer trade among member countries, whilst still maintaining their own trade barriers against non-member countries. For example, the signing of the North American Free Trade Agreement between US, Canada and Mexico has boosted trade in agricultural produce among these countries. Several years after the agreement came into effect, Mexico became US's 2nd largest export market for meat products.

In 2015, the World Trade Organisation agreed to eliminate $15 billion of subsidies on exported agricultural products from milk to sugar and rice. Countries like India and Thailand, whose governments have been providing such subsidies could see their agricultural exports fall, while countries like Australia, Canada and New Zealand whose farmers do not benefit from such subsidies may see a boost in agricultural exports.

Proximity

Transport costs might hinder trade from occurring according to the theory of comparative advantage. For example, although Peru may have the greatest comparative advantage in producing tuna, the high transport costs from Peru to Singapore means that it will be more expensive to import from Peru than to import from nearby neighbours like Malaysia and Indonesia. Transport cost is a factor which explains why Singapore imports large volumes of food from her neighbouring countries rather than faraway countries with the lowest opportunity cost. Hence, a country's pattern of trade can be influenced by the geographical accessibility and distance between her and her trading partners.

Evaluation

Among all the factors above, comparative advantage is probably still the most important factor affecting the pattern of trade since it forms the basis for trade and how gains from trade arise. Government policies also do affect the pattern of trade very significantly. For example, through various supply side policies, the Singapore Government has developed comparative advantages in the Biomedical and Petrochemical sectors, which are Singapore's key export sectors today. Government policies to pursue FTAs also have significant impact on the pattern of trade. For example, the US-Singapore FTA has also been credited with boosting total trade between Singapore and the US by 53%, ten years after signing the agreement. In contrast, US and Asia trade only grew by 42% during the same period. Therefore, since the USSFTA, both have become even more significant trade partners.

46. Explain the benefits of trade.

Foremost, trade **provides access to more markets**, increasing **demand for domestically produced goods and services**. As export revenue (X) and net exports (X-M) increase, AD increases from AD_1 to AD_2 in Fig 1. This will cause an **unplanned decrease in the stocks and inventories** of domestic producers. They will hence **hire more workers to increase production**. Via the multiplier effect, this will result in **a multiplied increase in real GDP from Y_1 to Y_2** and hence there is actual growth. As firms increase production to meet the increased demand, there is increased derived demand for factors of production such as labour, hence **reducing unemployment**.

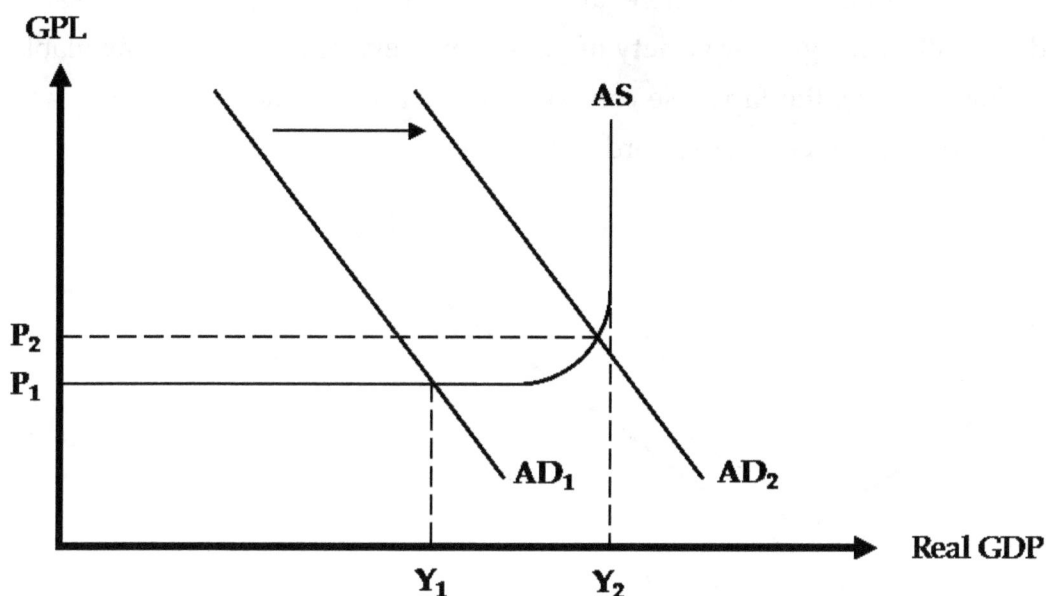

Fig 1: Increased AD from Trade

As countries experience actual growth, their demand for normal goods and services will increase. Hence, they will tend to import more, leading to further trade. As the amount of trade among the economies increase, it results in further growth. Hence, engaging in trade can result in a virtuous cycle of increased trade and higher economic growth.

An extended market can also allow firms to expand their scale of production to achieve internal economies of scale, thereby achieving lower unit costs of production (COP) in the long-run.

With the removal or reduction of trade barriers, producers are **exposed to greater competition** and come **under pressure to be as efficient as possible** in order to **remain competitive** in the global market. **This competitiveness ensures lower prices** for consumers which results in **gain in consumer welfare. As prices fall, households can also consume more goods and services. Therefore, standard of living (SOL) increases.**

As competition increases, producers will also seek to innovate and improve the quality of their goods and services. Consumers will thus **benefit also from higher quality goods and services.**

Furthermore, in the global market, there are many different variants of the same product. Trade can allow for **greater variety of goods and services** to be made available to consumers. For example, the Japanese can consume not just Honda or Toyota cars, but can also buy BMWs from Germany, Ford from the US and Hyundai from Korea etc.

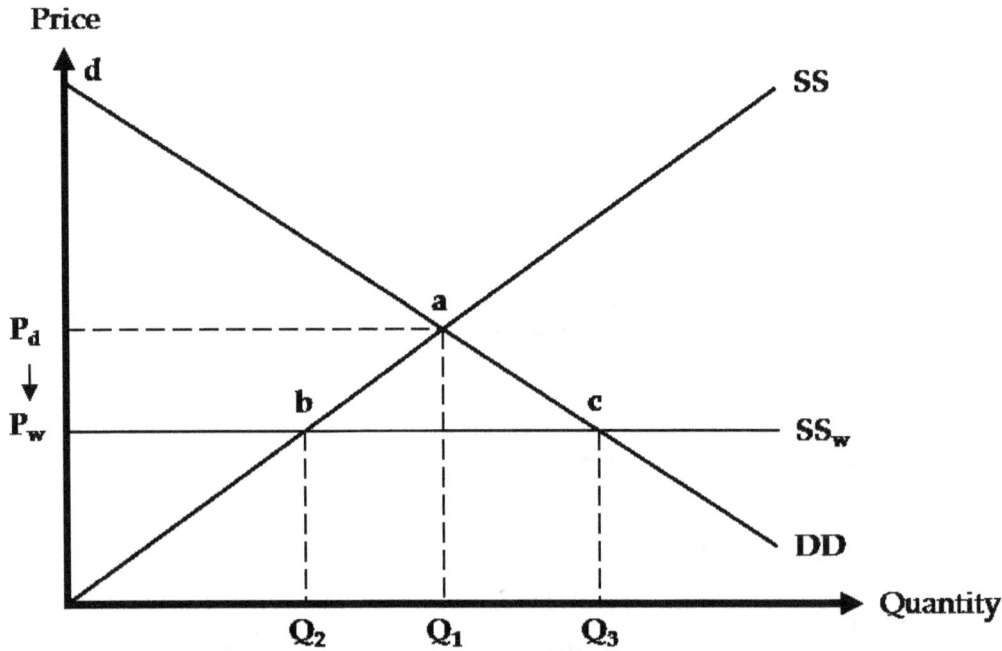

Fig 2: Textile Market in USA

Referring to Fig 2, DD represents domestic demand while SS represents domestic supply in the fabrics market in USA. Initially, USA produces at the equilibrium quantity of Q_1 at the equilibrium price of P_d.

However, when USA is **open to trade**, supply for fabrics in the US becomes the world supply, SS_w, at the prevailing world price of P_w below domestic price P_d. **SS_w is assumed to be perfectly price elastic, meaning that at prevailing world price P_w, an infinite amount can be supplied.** With trade, domestic producers are **exposed to intense competition**. Domestic firms have to also **sell at the lower price** of P_w and produce at Q_2 instead. Hence, **consumer surplus increases** from daP_d to dcP_w as consumer prices fall and **consumption increases** from Q_1 to Q_3. There is an increase in social surplus, resulting in a societal welfare gain of area abc as a result of more efficient global allocation of resources.

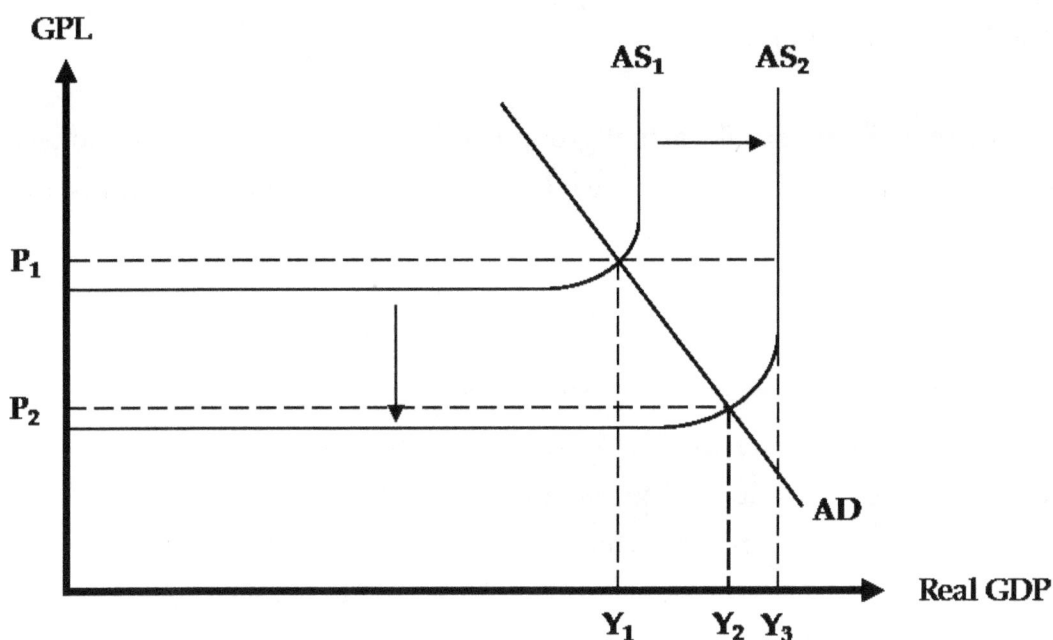

Fig 3: Increased AS from Trade

Additionally, firms **can import factor inputs** from **cheaper foreign sources and this lowers their unit COP and increases short-run aggregate supply (SRAS).** At the same time, trade allows for the import of better capital goods that are made with new, cutting-edge technology. This will result in **more efficient, sophisticated techniques of production** that can produce more output with fewer resources. This will increase the economy's productive capacity and long-run aggregate supply (LRAS).

The combined increase in SRAS and LRAS results in an outward shift in AS curve from AS_1 to AS_2 in Fig 3, as firms are willing and able to produce more at each general price level (GPL) and there is greater spare capacity for utilisation of resources for greater level of production. In order to increase real output, firms will have to hire more workers to increase output, made possible only by the increased spare capacity. Hence, real national output increases from Y_1 to Y_2 and greater levels of employment are achieved. This reflects **actual growth** in the economy. Furthermore, the lower COP will result in **lower cost-push inflationary pressures** as firms pass on cost savings to consumers. At the same time, the increased spare capacity and full employment level from Y_1 to Y_3 reduces competition for scarce factors of production, helping ease demand-pull inflationary pressures as firms also pass on these cost savings to consumers. Both of these effects contribute to the overall lower inflationary pressure, resulting in a fall in GPL from P_1 to P_2.

As such, the increase in SRAS enables actual growth and reduces cost-push inflationary pressures, while the increase in LRAS reduces demand-pull inflationary pressures and ensures long-term sustainable economic growth.

> **Tip**
> The benefits of trade are not the same as the benefits of free trade. Benefits of free trade refer to benefits derived from trading with the rest of the world without trade barriers, while benefits of trade merely refer to the benefits of trading with another particular country. The benefits of free trade are greater than the benefits of trade.

Evaluation

Vulnerability to External Shocks – Fall in External Demand

However, countries that are open to free trade will be **more vulnerable to other countries' economic crises**. These shocks **can be transmitted from one country to another through various channels, resulting in trade and financial spillovers**. For example, with recession in USA, income of the Americans fell which led to a fall in demand for goods and services which included that of Vietnam's exports. With net exports falling, Vietnam's AD fell and thus led to a multiplied fall in national income through the multiplier effect, resulting in increased cyclical unemployment.

Hence, it is **important for economies to diversify their export markets** and have **more trading partners** so that when one trading partner experiences a sudden economic downturn, there are other **trading partners that still provide a source of external demand**. The ideal is to have trading partners from various regions of the world, so that when one region is experiencing sharp economic downturn, other regions of the world **may be on a different stage of the business cycle**. These economies may be experiencing a boom and will **continue to contribute to export growth.**

Vulnerability to External Shocks – Imported Inflation

Furthermore, trade increases susceptibility to imported inflation. As prices of world commodities like oil rise, countries importing these commodities will be affected by these increased prices and "import" this inflation.

Vulnerability to Structural Unemployment

Additionally, rapid changes in comparative advantage can cause massive structural unemployment. For example, the **US has lost comparative advantage in labour intensive manufacturing due to the emergence of low-cost economies like China and India.** These economies possess greater factor endowment of cheap labour and hence have comparative advantage in producing low-end, low-skilled labour intensive goods. As such, these industries in the US have declined and firms have relocated to economies like China and India. Many workers who are unemployed may lack skills to work in the new sectors with comparative advantage such as ecommerce, and thus become structurally unemployed.

Nevertheless, despite these potentially detrimental consequences, it must be acknowledged that the **benefits of extended markets, lower prices and greater efficiency far outweigh** the susceptibility to imported inflation, "imported recession" and structural unemployment. This is especially true for small and open economies (SOEs) like Singapore where the limited domestic demand is insufficient to drive economic growth. If Singapore were to rely on domestic demand, the level of employment and SOL achieved would be so low that it would be worse than a trading Singapore experiencing an "imported recession".

Ultimately, **trade must be viewed as a virtue and free trade be undertaken as much as possible**. In order to guard against potential detriments, countries should **diversify their trading partners** and export markets to better guard against "imported recession". In order to prevent massive structural unemployment or economic downturn due to a loss in comparative advantage, countries should continually invest in education and retraining to ensure workers continually remain relevant in an ever-changing global economy. More research and development can also be conducted so that when one industry loses comparative advantage, there can be new industries with comparative advantage to drive economic growth.

47. Explain how tariffs work to achieve macroeconomic goals.

A tariff is a **tax** levied on imports. Usually, governments levy tariffs on imports to **protect the domestic economy** from foreign competition, thereby **reducing the loss of jobs**. The government also levies tariffs to **correct a Balance of Trade (BOT) deficit** or **boost economic growth** through import substitution.

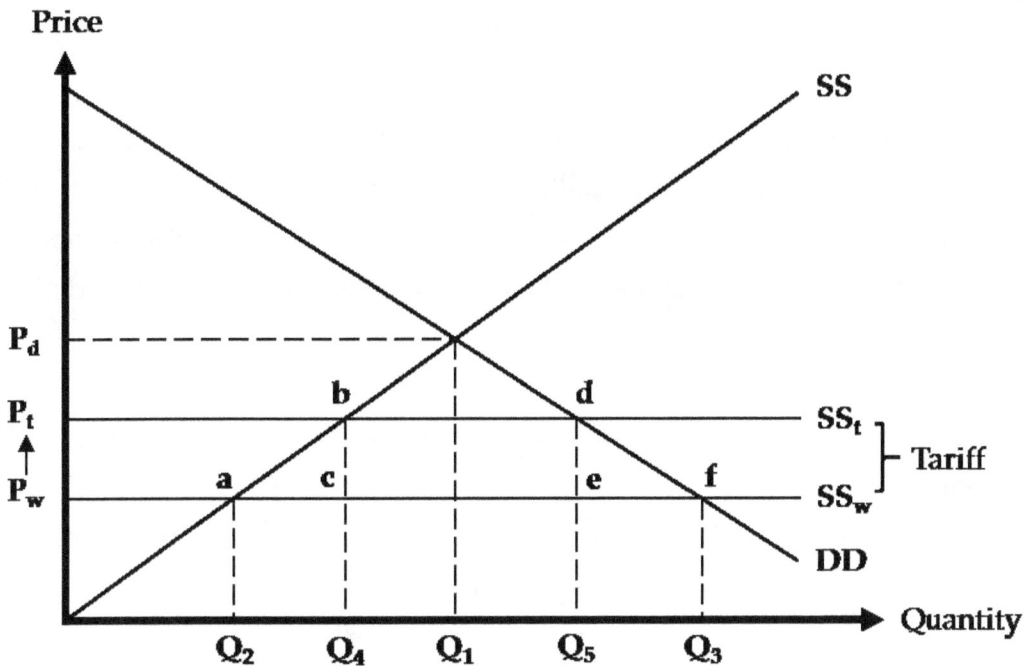

Fig 1: Fabrics Market in USA

Referring to Fig 1, DD represents domestic demand while SS represents domestic supply in the fabrics market in USA. Initially without trade, USA produces at the equilibrium quantity of Q_1 at the equilibrium price of P_d.

However, as USA becomes **open to trade**, it is able to import at the prevailing world price P_w. It is assumed that **world supply SS_w is perfectly price elastic** and at the prevailing P_w, an infinite amount of imports can be obtained. At the world price P_w, Q_3 of textiles is demanded while domestic producers are only willing to produce Q_2 of textiles, resulting **a fall in output of Q_2Q_1.** The fall in output means that domestic producers **will lay off workers, which results in increased unemployment.**

The US government may choose to **impose a tariff on textiles** and world supply for textiles hence shifts upwards from SS_w to SS_t. As a result of this tariff, price of textiles increases from P_w to P_t. At this higher price, the quantity demanded for imports will fall from Q_2Q_3 to Q_4Q_5, while quantity consumed falls from Q_3 to Q_5. Consumers will switch their expenditure towards domestically produced goods and services. **Domestic producers are also willing to produce more textiles at the higher price**, and will hence **increase production** from Q_2 to Q_4. In increasing production, these firms will **hire more workers** and hence, **employment will increase.**

Additionally, due to the imposition of tariffs, the government earns tax revenue of area bced. This contributes to government budget, allowing the government to better engage in expansionary fiscal policy if need be, as well as increasing its ability to redistribute income in the form of increased welfare payments or tax rebates to the unemployed and lower income groups.

Furthermore, import expenditure (M) will fall, increasing net exports (X-M) and improving the Balance of Trade (BOT). Thus aggregate demand (AD) and real GDP will increase by a multiplied amount via the multiplier effect. As such, **actual growth is achieved while the Balance of Payments (BOP) improves**.

Hence, tariffs can prevent high rates of unemployment by protecting the domestic textile industry from foreign competition, boosting economic growth and improving BOP position, while increasing the government's ability for expansionary fiscal policy and income redistribution.

Evaluation

However, by limiting imports, other countries, namely trading partners of the country practicing protectionism, will experience a fall in their export revenue. As such, this may adversely affect their economic growth and may even lead to a decline in economic activity due to a fall in (X-M) leading to a fall in AD. **In the long-run, this could result in a fall in demand for the exports of the country imposing protectionism given that its trading partners experience lower incomes and sluggish economic growth. As a** result, worsening of BOP and a slowdown in economic growth may be experienced. This is known as the beggar-thy-neighbour effect.

Furthermore, this **could lead to retaliation** by trading partners since their economies are adversely affected. Hence, they may counter by imposing their own forms of protectionism. For example, if they impose tariffs, now the initial country's exports become less price competitive and this can result in a fall in export revenue (X), offsetting any prior improvement in the trade balance. It can also lead to a **fall in economic growth** and **increased unemployment** since **X will decrease** given protectionism imposed by trading partners.

Additionally, the effectiveness of tariffs **depend on price elasticity of demand for imports.** If there is a lack of domestic substitutes, there would be a less than proportionate fall in quantity demanded for imports despite the higher post tariff price, therefore the tariff will not be effective in reducing M.

If the imports are factor inputs, this may lead to an increase in the unit costs of production for sectors that require these inputs. Even if these sectors were to purchase factor inputs domestically, this would most likely be more expensive than what the imports cost initially. Hence sectors requiring these inputs may face higher costs, and become less price competitive.

Tariffs can also **breed productive inefficiency** as firms are sheltered from foreign competition. Firms may continue producing via methods that incur higher costs of production than necessary. This is especially pertinent for countries where tariffs were enacted to protect infant industries in the hope of these industries acquiring the necessary internal economies of scale and price competitiveness to compete on the global market in the long term. Due to the tariffs, infant industries may remain as "perpetual infants" as the protection reduces the incentive for any investments in research, development and cost reduction. Hence, these industries may never acquire the price competitiveness required to compete in the global market.

Furthermore, tariffs can cause allocative inefficiency. By imposing tariffs, domestic producers are willing and able to produce more at Q_4, as opposed to Q_2 before. This increase in production represents an over-allocation of domestic resources towards the production of the good by Q_2Q_4, leading to a deadweight welfare loss of area abc. The decrease in quantity consumed by Q_5Q_3 also leads to a further deadweight welfare loss of area def, resulting in a total deadweight welfare loss of area abc + def.

Ultimately, while the costs of imposing a tariff are numerous, it is still a preferred method of protectionism given the **tax revenue** that can be obtained. This tax revenue can be used to **fund retraining programs** or to **exploit new areas of comparative advantage** so as to correct any BOP deficit and to improve export competitiveness, increasing economic growth and employment. For example, if a country is losing comparative advantage in the manufacturing sector, tariffs can be imposed on imports of similar manufacturing goods. The revenue obtained can then be used to invest in education and skills upgrading programs. This way, workers in the manufacturing industries can upgrade their skills, allowing the economy to move towards more knowledge-based and high-skilled industries. In contrast, other policies like hidden export subsidies are not sustainable in the long-run as it draws down on government reserves which are, after all, finite.

48. Explain the implications of a small and open economy.

A small and open economy (SOE) has several defining characteristics that make them less resilient and limit their policy options in influencing the level of economic activity. Foremost, SOEs **have a small domestic market due to a small population size.** This tends to result in SOEs being very export-dependent and FDI-reliant for economic growth. SOEs are also geographically small countries, and hence they tend to **lack natural resources** and have to import many factor inputs.

Furthermore, SOEs tend to have **no control over interest rate (i/r)**. They are usually very open to capital flows due to the need to finance the large volumes of trading activities and due to dependence on FDI. Being small players in the global market, they are unable to influence the global i/r and are i/r takers instead of i/r setters. If they choose to **increase i/r,** this will result in large amounts of **hot money inflows**, made possible because of openness of capital flows, which will increase money supply in the economy. This will drive down i/r again, cancelling out the initial increase in i/r. Therefore, i/r-centred monetary policy is not feasible for SOEs.

Because of these characteristics, small and open economies **cannot rely on the domestic market to drive economic growth**, and are **hence very export-oriented economies** with a strong emphasis on **export competitiveness and comparative advantage**. In a global recession, these economies tend to **be more adversely affected** as they are less able to turn to the domestic market to cushion an economic downturn. Certain policy options are therefore most effective while others are less effective.

Fiscal policy is less effective for SOEs given **that consumption (C) and domestic demand take up a small proportion of aggregate demand (AD) and real GDP.** Even if domestic demand is stimulated, it only comprises a **small proportion of AD** and hence AD will not be increased as much as compared to in the case of a larger economy. For example, Singapore's C to GDP ratio stands at 40% as compared to USA, which is a large and less open economy and stands at 70%, underscoring the lower efficacy of fiscal policy in Singapore. Furthermore, SOEs have a **high marginal propensity to import** due to their heavy dependence on imports arising from lack of natural resources. Hence, ceteris paribus, they tend to experience a higher marginal propensity to withdraw and a lower size of the multiplier. To this end, the initial stimulus from government spending **will not result in a large multiplied increase** in AD and real GDP as compared to a larger economy.

I/r-centred monetary policy is **completely ineffective** for SOEs that **are also highly open to capital flows**, such as Singapore. Their **inability to control i/r** means that other policy options need to be explored. For SOEs that do practice certain forms of capital controls, even an expansionary monetary policy by lowering i/r will **not result in a large increase in AD** since domestic demand is a small proportion of AD, and the multiplier is small.

Protectionism is not recommended for SOEs since they are **reliant on exports for growth and imports for raw materials**. Enacting protectionism could invite **retaliation** and hence potentially cut off any larger markets that these economies could exploit. This is especially harmful to SOEs since **they cannot turn to their domestic market to drive economic growth** in the face of retaliation from trading partners. In comparison, larger open economies can still afford to rely on domestic demand to boost economic growth. Furthermore, SOEs tend to lack natural resources and are import-reliant. Protectionism will therefore disrupt its production and increase its unit costs of production. Hence, protectionism is not a sensible policy option for SOEs.

Exchange rate (e/r)-centred monetary policy is **especially effective** for SOEs since they are so trade dependent. E/r policy can directly influence the level of exports and this can be especially effective as export revenue (X) makes up a large proportion of GDP. In the event of an economic downturn, a depreciation would increase export price competitiveness and hence increase net exports (X-M) and AD, thereby mitigating the effects of the recession. The ability to control e/r also means that the price of imports in domestic currency can be controlled. Controlling imported inflation is especially important as SOEs are highly import-dependent for factor inputs and for consumption, making imported inflation a key source of inflation for SOEs. An appreciation would lower price of imports in domestic currency, reducing imported inflation.

Trade policies in the form of free trade agreements (FTAs) are highly suitable for SOEs. As SOEs are highly dependent on exports for growth, signing FTAs **opens up more export markets** and hence **ensures greater X**, driving AD and actual growth. It also helps to **ensure that SOEs will not fall victim to protectionism** that may be enacted by trading partners in future.

SOEs' reliance on exports also means that **export-price competitiveness is very important** to achieve economic growth. In order to ensure export-price competitiveness, **short-run supply-side policies** can be employed as they **lower the unit cost of production** and hence ensure that **exports are cheaper**. This will **increase the quantity demanded of exports and hence increase X and AD**, leading to actual growth.

Furthermore, because of a **lack of natural factor endowments**, SOEs need to **continually develop new areas of comparative advantage** to **ensure export price and non-price competitiveness**. For example, Singapore has invested significantly in developing infant industries where we have potential to achieve comparative advantage in. Long-run supply-side policies are needed to develop these new industries. For example, the government has developed extensive infrastructure in the form of Jurong Island, Fusionopolis, Biopolis in order to develop the petrochemical and biomedical industries. In addition, various tax incentives are used to attract FDI into these sectors. Specific training and education programmes are also developed in order to develop the necessary skills needed for these sectors. Therefore, long-run supply-side policies are usually of great importance to SOEs to ensure long-term sustainable economic growth.

Finally, SOEs are especially vulnerable to external shocks due to heavy dependence on trade. Recessions overseas are very likely to also lead to the SOE experiencing one, since demand for exports would be falling and exports take up the largets pro[ortion of its Real GDP. This will in turn lead to higher cyclical unemployment. Likewise should there be rising prices overseas, for example, due to supply shocks in oil and commodity markets, SOEs will likely end up importing the inflation.

49. Explain how globalisation may lead to more structural unemployment.

Globalization refers to the greater interconnectedness between economies as a result of freer flow of goods and services, capital, labour, technology, knowledge and ideas between countries.

With globalization, **more cost-competitive countries** that possess comparative advantage in certain areas of production requiring abundance of low-skilled labour may emerge. As such, **countries may end up losing comparative advantage** in areas like labour-intensive manufacturing and this will result in the **shutting down and relocation of firms to the other countries**, increasing unemployment. Countries that have lost comparative advantage in labour intensive manufacturing may **restructure their economies towards other more high-end, high value-added sectors of production**. However, retrenched workers may not possess the skills necessary to work in these sectors. There is hence a **mismatch between the skills required and the skills that workers possess**. Thus, structural unemployment occurs.

For example, in the past, **US possessed comparative advantage in textiles and consumer electronics**. However, due to the **emergence of low-cost economies like China and India** which possess greater factor endowment of cheap labour, firms shut down and relocated from US to China and India in order to capitalize on lower labour costs there. As these labour-intensive manufacturing industries in the US declined, retrenched workers found themselves unable to move into **sunrise industries** like the knowledge-intensive IT sector **due to a lack of the necessary skills**.

50. Explain how globalisation may help reduce inflation.

Globalization refers to the greater interconnectedness between economies as a result of freer flow of goods and services, capital, labour, technology, knowledge and ideas between countries. Globalization can help reduce inflation through either increasing the short-run aggregate supply (SRAS) or the long-run aggregate supply (LRAS).

Firstly, globalization allows for **greater access to foreign resources** like capital, technology, and labour, resulting in an increase in aggregate supply (AS). **Greater access to foreign sources of raw materials** allow for the import of factor inputs that are **cheaper than domestic alternatives**. Firms can experience a **fall in the cost of production (COP)** by **importing cheaper factor inputs**. These cost savings will then translate into an increase in the SRAS resulting in lower general price levels (GPL).

With globalization, countries can now more easily obtain foreign technology and capital goods, thereby resulting in more sophisticated and efficient methods of production. This can result in a **fall in the unit COP hence increasing SRAS.** Foreign technology and capital goods will also allow for an increase in a country's quality and quantity of resources. This will **increase a country's productive capacity and hence increase LRAS.**

Increased labour flows **allow countries to experience an influx of cheaper foreign labour**. This **curbs wage-push inflation** as low-wage foreign workers can be quite easily employed instead of giving in to the wage demands of local workers. Thus the bargaining power of trade unions may also be curtailed. Cheaper labour also means that unit COP falls as labour is a key factor of production, hence increasing SRAS. The influx of migrants also helps augment the domestic workforce, thus increasing the quantity of labour and the productive capacity and hence increasing LRAS.

The influx of skilled foreign workers can also contribute to increasing productivity. This will drive down unit labour costs, further increasing SRAS. Concurrently, these foreign workers will augment the labour force, increasing the quantity and quality of labour with their knowledge and experience, hence increasing LRAS.

GPL

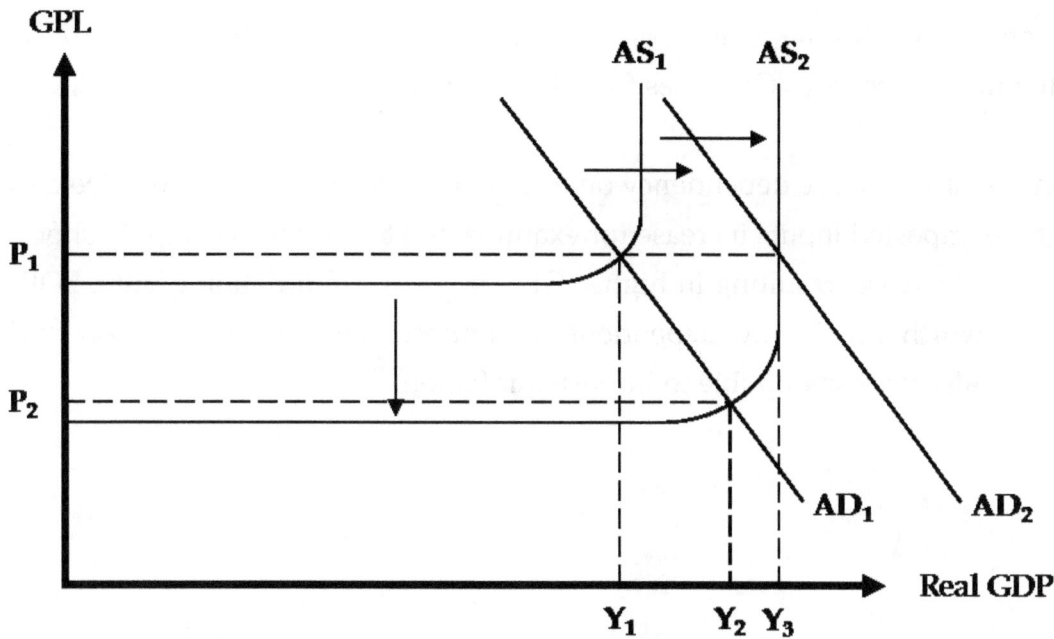

Fig 1: Inflation from Globalisation

The combined increase in SRAS and LRAS from globalisation results in increase in AS from AS_1 to AS_2 in Fig 1. The increased SRAS stems from a lower unit COP due to cheaper factor inputs, greater labour productivity and more efficient technology, hence lowering cost-push inflationary pressures as firms pass on cost savings to consumers. The increased LRAS stems from increased quality and quantity of labour provided by foreign labour as well as foreign technology, increasing the amount of spare capacity available in the economy. This reduces competition for scarce factors of production, lowering demand-pull inflationary pressures as firms pass on cost savings to consumers. The combined effects of higher SRAS and LRAS hence results in an overall reduced inflationary pressure as GPL falls from P_1 to P_2. As such, globalisation allows for long-term sustainable economic growth by enabling both actual and potential growth.

<u>Evaluation</u>

However, globalization can also increase inflation. Globalization could lead to hot money inflows, increasing money supply and lowering interest rates. This could stimulate excessive borrowing, increasing consumption (C), increasing AD. Increasing X due to the increased export markets as well as increasing C due to an influx of immigrants can also contribute to increasing AD. If AD increases from AD_1 to AD_2, demand-pull inflation occurs as GPL rises from P_2 back to P_1.

Globalization can also increase dependency on imported inputs such as oil and steel. As the price of these imported inputs increase for example due to an external supply shock, the unit COP will increase, resulting in higher GPL as cost-push inflation occurs. SOEs and economies which are highly dependent on imports for both production and consumption are also very susceptible to imported inflation.